Simple puppetry

Simple puppetry

Sheila Jackson

Studio Vista London
Watson-Guptill Publications New York

General Editors Janey O'Riordan and Brenda Herbert
© Sheila Jackson 1969
Published in London by Studio Vista Limited
Blue Star House, Highgate Hill, London N19
and in New York by Watson-Guptill Publications
165 West 46th Street, New York 10036
Library of Congress Catalog Card Number 72-79565
Distributed in Canada by General Publishing Co. Ltd
30 Lesmill Road, Don Mills, Toronto, Canada
Set in Univers 9 on 9½ pt
Printed and bound in Great Britain by
Bookprint Limited, Crawley, Sussex

SBN 289 79584 2

Contents

For Gladys and Laurence Steele

1 Introduction

This book deals with the principles of simple puppet making, covering the three main methods – glove (hand) puppets, rod puppets, and string puppets, or marionettes. The instructions for making each puppet usually culminate in some particular character, but this need only be regarded as one of the many possibilities open to the designer, and the methods described will be helpful in building up other figures. Many of the processes involved in one puppet could often be used in the making of a different type; different kinds of joints, different ways of fixing parts together, and a variety of materials will be found to be interchangeable. Therefore it is a good idea to browse through the book before getting to work on one particular subject.

Sometimes, especially for the entertainment of small children, the making of a single puppet is the object, and in this instance the choice of character depends on the maker and the interests and age of the potential owner. The result is really an animated toy which may well kindle interest, leading later to participation in puppet theatre activities.

The conception of puppets as a dramatic activity is quite different. It is a mistake to design the puppet before knowing exactly what it is going to do; its shape and proportion need to be built around certain requirements. If the basic needs are first settled on, other incidental movements will follow later. In this way it will be seen that the functional necessities to some extent govern the appearance of the puppet and the design will develop out of these limitations. It is the limitations which give puppets their individuality and charm, they demand imagination and inventiveness of their creators and reward this with a vigorous quality of their own. They must never be regarded as little people or miniature actors, for they are neither of these things, and for this reason special kinds of plays and entertainments need to be conceived for them.

Start by deciding whether you are going to work with gloves (hands), rods or strings. This needs plenty of consideration, for the method used influences the kind of productions you will be able to do; if working with very young children string puppets can be very frustrating, with older groups the limitations imposed by glove or hand puppets can be equally tiresome. For students and adult groups the decision between rods and strings is purely an aesthetic one, and it is often a good idea to make one or two of each and to experiment with these before making a final decision. Glove (hand) puppets and rod puppets can be combined in the same production, but the difference in staging necessary for string puppets makes the combination of these with any other variety rather a problem.

Determine the size of the puppets at the outset. This does not mean that they will not vary – tall ones, short ones, fat ones etc all combine to make up the puppet show, but a basic size must be chosen on which to plan. With glove (hand) puppets the size is governed by the manipulator's hand, but with rod and string puppets there is much more flexibility. Most people start by making puppets too small, and this may present problems in operation and also in the selection of suitable materials for cos-tuming and for scenery; the scale of materials for dressing puppets is very important and if the figures are very tiny most fabrics and trimmings are too coarse and bulky, which not only looks bad, but also impedes the movements. String puppets which are too light in weight are difficult to operate, rod puppets which are too heavy soon make the arms ache. Some experiment will help to decide on a size agreeable to the operators and suitable to the kind of stage available.

Some thought as to where the puppets are going to perform should be considered at this point. In suitable weather an open window can form a theatre; glove (hand) and rod puppets can be manipulated from a kneeling position, with a screen behind them on which scenery is pinned; string puppeteers can stand on a table and work over a screen with the puppets using a wide window sill as a stage floor; or a clothes-horse (a collapsible rack for drying clothes) or table can be ingeniously converted into a theatre.

This is fine to begin with, but keen performers will soon be thinking in terms of a simple stage set-up such as one of those described later for glove and rod puppets (the rather more com-plicated construction of a marionette theatre is beyond the scope of this book), and it is with this in mind that the final decision must be made. The amount of space available for performance and storage is unfortunately often a deciding factor. The outlay for a theatre need not be very great, for hardboard and wooden battens (thin strips of wood) are not costly, and in the early stages the cost of the puppets themselves is negligible as they can be created from all kinds of scraps and junk, and it is only as the maker becomes more experienced and ambitious in design that special materials need be bought; even then it is often the puppets made ingeniously on a shoe string which prove most successful.

Although this book deals exclusively with the practical and

visual side of the puppet stage, this is only part of the creation of a complete puppet theatre. Very full consideration must be given to the musical and dramatic side of the production, and the visual side must interpret this creatively. It is best to start simply with little episodes involving only two puppets, exploring the possibilities of their actions and wedding these to music, speech or commentary. Nursery rhymes, poems and songs are excellent for first ventures; moving puppets to music is very helpful as it teaches operators to move them rhythmically. Practise moving them in front of a mirror, but remember it is essential to get the feel as well as the look of their movements. In certain circumstances it may be necessary to have two operators to one puppet, or, in the case of rod puppets, to have two identical puppets made in such a way that they perform different actions although they look like the same puppet to the audience.

Only after exhaustive practice and rehearsal, when both operators and stage managers are really proficient, has the time come to give a show.

Tools and materials

Only a few simple tools are needed for most of the puppets described in this book, and most of them anyone in the habit of doing craftwork is likly to have already. Some brown paper, or better still, squared or graph paper, should be kept available for drawing out patterns. As many of the patterns given in this book are drawn half-size they can easily be enlarged to full size by taking measurements with a pair of compasses (fig. 1e) or dividers, and doubling them.

Tool requirements are listed before each set of instructions, and the drawings in this section show most of those mentioned. Fig. 1. Two good pairs of scissors are essential for all work, a medium cutting-out pair (i) and a small pair of embroidery scissors for cutting intricate shapes such as felt trimmings (j). A ruler, preferably with a metal cutting edge, is a necessity. A Stanley (mat) knife, which has removable blades (b), is invaluable for cutting out shapes, trimming, and a multitude of other purposes. Pliers will be needed for bending and cutting wire, and the type with the pointed nose are the most useful for puppet-making, (a). An awl (n), which costs very little, will be found very useful for making holes in various kinds of plastic containers after the point has been heated in a flame. A bradawl (m)

9

Fig. 1

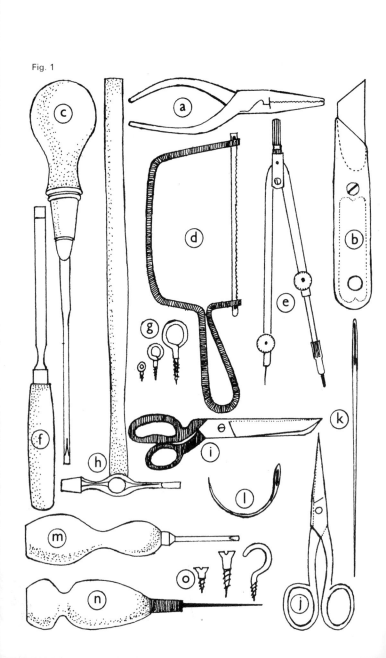

Fig. 2

makes holes in wood ready for the insertion of screws, screw eyes and cup hooks. A screwdriver (c) will be needed by those who set about building a puppet theatre. A hack saw (d) is not only useful for cutting off nails but also, being small in size, can be conveniently used for cutting dowel and small square-sectioned pieces of wood. A tack hammer (h) is another tool often useful in puppetry. Various sized screw eyes are shown (g) – tiny copper or brass ones suitable for inserting into legs, arms and hands to take strings; medium ones, best for shoulders and back strings and also for use in controls, large ones which may be used in the neck cavity of wooden puppets. Small screws or a cup hook (o) are often inserted in the top of a control to facilitate hanging up. The long needle (k) is an upholstery needle to be used when working on stuffed puppets. A curved needle (l) is useful when working on awkward shapes.

Fig. 2. Various brushes will be needed for gluing and painting; the minimum selection would be a one-inch brush (p), a large-sized sable (q) and a brush with a fine point (r). It is false economy to buy cheap brushes. Keep them clean by first using the requisite solvent and then rinsing in soapy water. Finally use clean cold water. Bulldog clips in various sizes are extremely useful for holding work together after it has been glued (s) and (t).

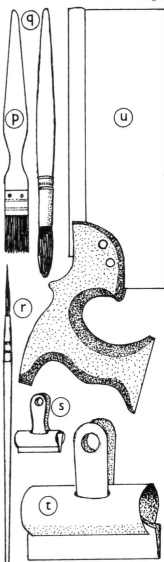

11

The tenon or back saw (u) is for cutting hardboard and battens (thin strips of wood) in building a theatre and for some scenery. Fig. 3. For wooden marionettes a drill (v) is a necessity but it is also helpful for many other jobs; (v1) shows the chuck into which various sized bits are fitted; (y1) is a spade drill. A file (x) is used for many smoothing jobs, as is sandpaper which is best if wrapped round a block of wood (x1). A very useful hook is shown (z); it is made from strong wire and can be used for hanging puppets or partly made pieces so as to keep them off the work table

If possible, have a special place to work with a strong bench or table having a surface on which to cut. Tools are best hung on a piece of pegboard within easy reach. Also close at hand there should be some shelves on which to store boxes containing nails, screw eyes, carpet and button thread etc. Larger boxes or calico bags should hold materials and trimmings; if beads and buttons are stored in screw-top glass containers or perspex (plexiglass) boxes their contents may be easily seen. Finally, always keep a good stock of various adhesives or glues, as it is very frustrating to run out in the middle of a job. Methylated (alcohol) and white (mineral) spirit, and thinners for other types of paint and glue, are essential to facilitate cleaning-up operations.

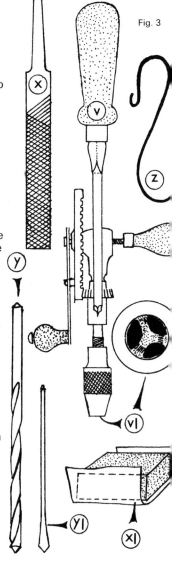

Fig. 3

2 Glove or hand puppets

Fig. 4

Most people have watched a Punch and Judy show in their childhood and enjoyed the robust action and humour. Many children immediately wish to imitate the performance themselves and a little encouragement and guidance from parents or teachers will start them off on a very creative enterprise, which can develop over the years as the children's experience develops.

The glove or hand puppet is the very simplest form of puppet, and is the best introduction to puppetry either at school or at home. As only the most basic materials are required there is a minimal outlay, and many homes will already have all that is necessary. A little organization and patience and a space to work will put the puppet theatre on its way.

Instructions are given in this chapter for a variety of glove (hand) puppets using various methods of construction which can be followed even if variations of style and character are being made; the patterns are intended as starting points for individual work and experiment. The felt puppet can be made by an adult for a tiny child, to whet the appetite and to act as a toy as much as a puppet.

These illustrations show Punch and Judy and a Devil, examples of Victorian glove or hand puppets. They have carved wood heads and hands. Punch has legs fixed to the front of the glove.

Fig. 5

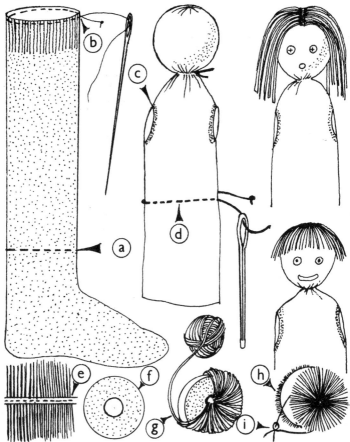

Sock puppets

Materials An old sock; thread; nail polish or latex (rubber-based) glue; beads or buttons and trimmings; round elastic; tape; wool (yarn), silk or string.

Tools Needle and bodkin (blunt needle); scissors.

Cut the sock as shown (a). Draw up the top of the sock with a thread (b). Run elastic around neck and stuff remainder of sock into the head, draw up the elastic and tie. Make two finger holes (c), smearing edges with nail polish or latex (rubber-based) glue to prevent fraying. Insert a piece of elastic to coincide with

Fig. 6

wrist, forming the waist, (d). Strands of wool (yarn) or string sewn to tape will make a wig (e); or cut 2 circles of cardboard (f), wind with wool (yarn) (g), then cut around edge (h) and tie tightly at centre (i). Ideas for characters are shown in fig. 6. They show a Bride, Groom, Bride's Mother and Clergyman. Spectacles can be made from a thin, pliable wire such as baling wire, or millinery wire. The bride's train is a plastic doily. Bits of feather, fur, artificial flowers, net etc will all be useful. Mittens worn under the glove look like sleeves.

Fig. 7

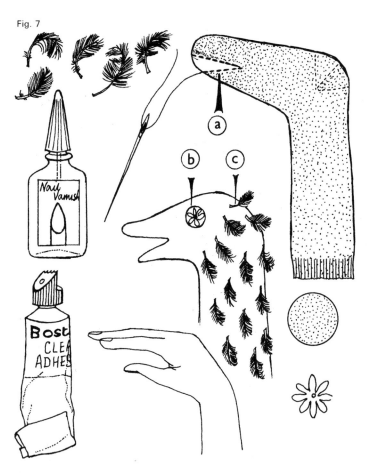

A BIRD FROM A SOCK

Materials Sock; contact adhesive (cement); nail polish; feathers; beads or sequins; felt circle; thread.

Tools Needle; scissors.

Make a V-shaped line of stitches (a), cut along line and smear with nail polish or latex (rubber-based) glue to prevent fraying. Turn sock inside out. Glue felt circle and sequin in place for eye (b). Glue feathers in place (c). For a more decorative bird, touch feathers with gold paint and spatter sequins among the feathers.

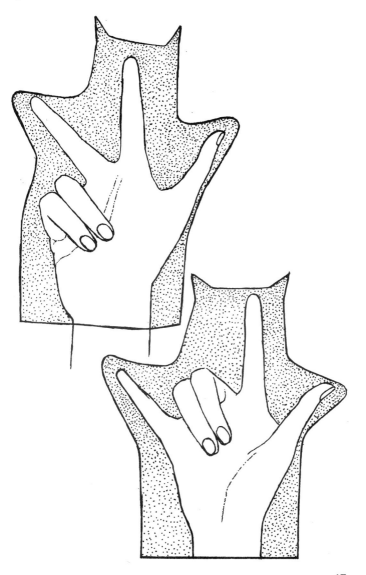

17

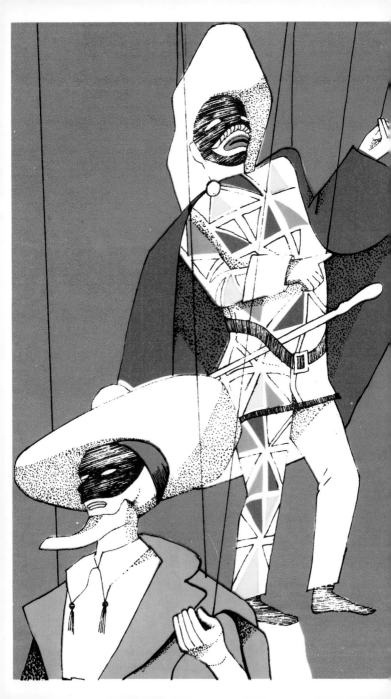

Owl: a child's puppet from felt

Materials Small quantities of felt in brown, grey and beige; two black sequins or beads for the eyes; Copydex, Sobo or similar latex (rubber-based) adhesive; sewing thread in the appropriate colours; paints – either poster paints or the acrylic type or emulsion paints will be suitable.

Tools A ruler or tape measure; a pair of compasses; pins; needles; a pair of scissors – embroidery scissors will help in cutting out finicky shapes and details; a paint brush with a good point.

This puppet is very pleasing when made from grey, brown and beige felts, with beady black pupils for the eyes. Fig. 10 shows an average-sized glove, but this can be easily adjusted to suit the size of the child's hand. The best way to do this is to draw round the hand when it is in the most comfortable operating position, see figs. 8 and 9. From this rough guide, draft the pattern and adjust the detail pieces so that they are in the same scale as in the design. The drawing is worked out to the scale of half an inch equals one inch. The pattern may first be drafted out on paper and then transferred to the felt or it may be drawn directly onto the felt.

Cut two pieces for the glove part of the puppet following the strong outline of the diagram, fig. 10 (a), placing the dotted line (a)–(b) on a fold of the material. Next cut two pieces each, (c) and (d), again placing the dotted line on the fold; these form the ruff round the neck of the bird, and should be notched with the scissors to form a fringe (e). Stitch these in place on the front and back parts of the glove (f).

Cut two wing pieces (g) and tack (baste) in place on the underside of the front half of the glove (h). For the eyes cut two pairs of circles, using different toned felts as (i) and (j), snipping round the edges to get a zig-zag effect. Placing the smaller circle on top of the larger circle, stitch into place on the front of the glove, at the same time placing a bead or sequin in position and stitching it in place to form the pupil of the eye. Either cut a snippet of felt (k) to suggest the beak or find a suitable bead and stitch or stick it into place.

Now put the back and front of the glove together and stitch them following the dotted line (m). This can be done on the right side of the glove, as with felt there is no need to have the seam on the inside. Small feathers of felt cut as (l) can be stuck on the owl's breast, and for more decorative effects they may be given a flick of either poster or acrylic paint.

19

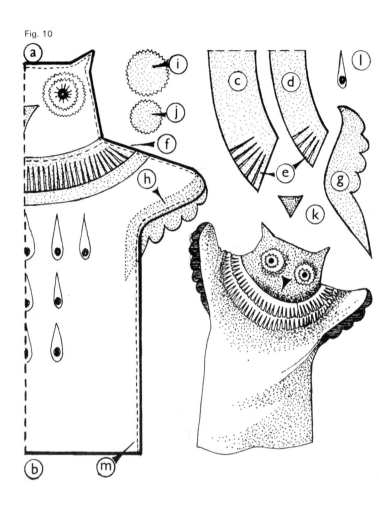

Fig. 10

Many simple glove (hand) puppets can be made by using this basic pattern and designing the shapes within the silhouette differently. Some suggestions for variations are shown on the following page. Although felt is very easy to use, all kinds of materials may be used successfully with very decorative results.

Fig. 11

For a cat puppet, the glove can be cut from felt as before, the stripes also cut from felt and glued in place with latex (rubber-based) glue, or painted and stencilled on to the glove (m). Pink felt circles make the paws (n). Eyes can be cut from felt, with sequin pupils. Cut a felt nose and embroider the mouth. Nylon bristles from a broom make the whiskers, fixed with a dab of contact adhesive (cement).

The pirate is slightly more complicated. Draft the basic shape, omitting the ears. Cut from striped material, or if a plain one is used, bands of braid or ribbon may be stitched on to it (r). Cut the hat shape double from black PVC (sheet plastic) or felt. Paint or appliqué the skull and cross-bones. Put aside for the moment. Cut in felt piece (c) from the owl pattern and fringe to make the beard (o). Cut shapes for the boots double, stitch and stuff lightly with foam rubber (p). Cut details for the face from scraps of felt and stick in place. Join the two sides of the glove. Stitch sides and top edges of hat, slip over top of head and sew in place. Attach boots to front of glove. Make a belt from PVC (sheet plastic), stitching in place at the side seams (q).

Finally a simple Punch. Proceed as for the other characters, keeping the shapes and colours simple. Small bells decorate the points of the collar.

Witch

Fig. 12

Materials Vinyl ball; short
length of dowel; thin cardboard;
cold water paste; newspaper;
two dish-cloths; contact adhesive
(cement); hairpins; twig; raffia; net.
Tools Awl; Stanley knife; paint
brushes; scissors; pins; needles;
thread.

Roll thin cardboard to form a tube
(a), and glue. With a knife shave
wooden dowel to make a nose
(b). Take a vinyl ball (d) of suitable size and make two holes in
it to take the nose peg and the
neck (c). This is done with the
point of an awl which has been
heated in a flame. Keep reheating
and revolve round the edges of
the hole until it is the right size.
Insert the nose and the neck.

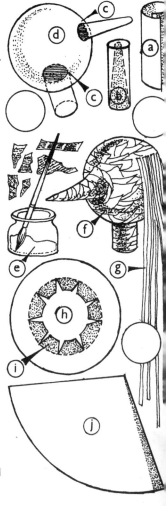

Now tear up a quantity of
newspaper into small pieces and
mix up some cold water paste
(such as flour paste) (e).
Paste the paper all over the
head, nose and neck (f), building
up the nose with extra pieces to
get a satisfactory shape, and
making sure that the join between
the ball and the neck is well
covered. Put aside to dry in a
warm place. Cut long strips of
thick paper or thin cardboard and
and stick onto the head to
form hair (g).

Cut the hat from cardboard
following the patterns (h) and
(j), bend the tabs (i) on the dotted
line. Join the edges of the conical
shape by gluing the dotted area
and pressing to its corresponding

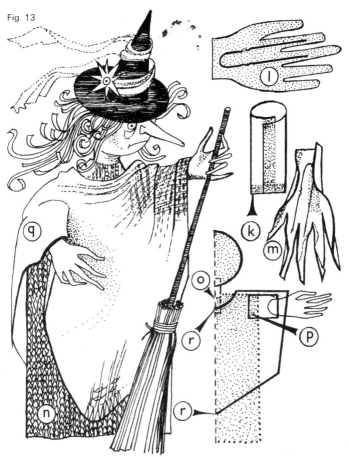

Fig. 13

edge. Glue the tabs of the brim and press inside the crown of the hat.

When dry glue the hat to the head. To make the hands follow fig. 13, cut the shape of the hands from thin cardboard (l) and glue a hairpin in place. Bend and twist the cardboard (m) to get the kind of shapes required and gently bend the hairpin to curve the fingers. Make two finger tubes (k) from thin cardboard and glue the dotted areas and press together. Glue the wrist of the hand to the closed end of the finger tube. Soak narrow strips of tissue paper in cold water paste and wind round the fingers, hand and and wrist to build up the shape. Put aside to dry. Take two dish-cloths of varying textures; reduce in size if necessary. In the first one (n) cut holes for the neck (o) and wrist and glue the hands in position (p) with contact adhesive (cement). Cut the cloak from the second dish-cloth following cutting line (r)–(r) in fig. 13. With the cloak (q) in place over the glove (n) insert the neck of the puppet into the neck opening and glue firmly in place. Now paint the witch with acrylic paints or with poster paints which, when dry, will need to be varnished. By drawing the back of a table knife against the strips of paper hair these can be effectively curled. Wind a whisp of net round the witch's hat and decorate with a star. A broomstick can be made to fit into one of the hands; for this use a twig or a thin length of dowel and bind strands of raffia to it.

Papier mâché heads

This is a very satisfactory way of making heads for glove or hand puppets for those who have some feeling for modelling. It is also very simple providing the processes are not rushed and sufficient time is left between the stages for drying out.

Modelling clay or plasticine may be used to build up the shape, from an egg-shaped lump worked round the end of a piece of broomstick (s). On to this gradually add pellets of clay until the character is arrived at. It is essential that the shapes should be kept simple (t). Next make some cold water paste and tear up a quantity of newspaper into pieces about one inch square. Grease the head all over with vaseline and then, with a soft brush, paste pieces of paper all over the head. Continue this process until there is a covering of at least six layers of paper, otherwise the papier mâché layer will be too thin and will collapse when the clay is removed.

Leave in a warm place until absolutely dry. Now cut round the head with a Stanley knife (u). If there are protuberances such as the ears shown in this case, cut into the plasticine with the blade so that this comes away with the papier mâché shell and ease the clay out of the ears with the point of the blade. The easing off of the shell needs to be done very gently and with great care, (v) and (w). Now glue the two halves together again by pasting two or three layers of paper pieces over the join (x). When the head is dry it is ready for painting.

Hands (z) and legs (y) can be made by exactly the same method.

Fig. 14

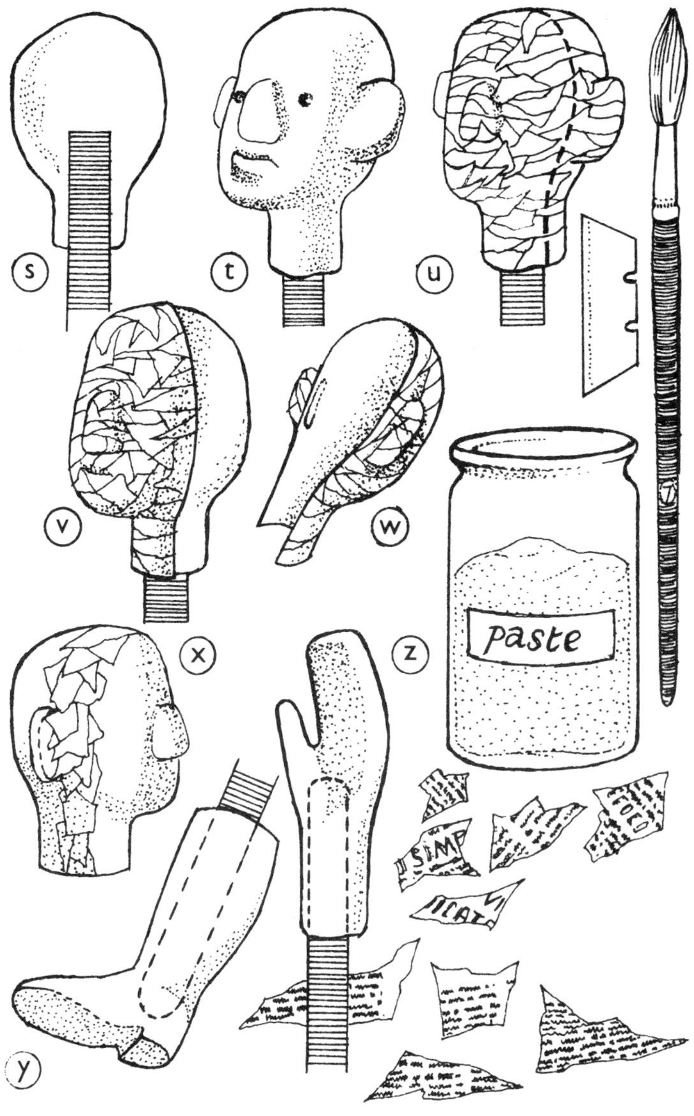

Latex heads

Find a cardboard box of a suitable size to hold the clay head with about one inch to spare on all sides (a). First mix up some plaster of Paris; use fine dental plaster which can usually be bought in England at a pharmacy, or a fine casting plaster which can be purchased from a supplier of sculpture materials. Put enough cold water in a basin and sift in the plaster until a mound appears above the water level (b). While still sifting with the left hand begin to mix the plaster with the right hand; the mixture needs to be about the consistency of whipping cream. Now pour into the box until it is nearly half full. Firmly place the head in the plaster, back downwards, until it is half submerged; this must be done with the minimum of wiggling. Allow to set. Revolve the blade of a blunt knife to make two registration holes (c). With a soft brush wetted and rubbed on to a cake of soap, thoroughly soap the now firm surface of the plaster. Clean the mixing bowl (this is most important) of all traces of plaster and proceed as before, filling up the top half of the box. Leave to set. Peel off the damp cardboard casing and gently work the two halves of the mould apart. Ease out the clay and brush out the mould with water. Drill a hole in the back of the mould to take a plastic funnel (d).

Liquid latex or moulding rubber

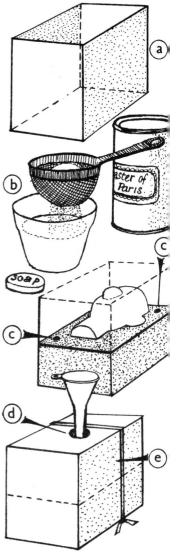

Fig. 15

Fig. 16

should be used to fill the mould. Place the two halves together – it is advisable to tie them with tape (e) – and leave near a stove or in a low oven until fairly hot, then completely fill the mould with latex or moulding rubber, pouring it into the hole through a funnel. Leave for about seven minutes, then pour any surplus liquid back into the can. This leaves the mould coated with the rubber, but hollow. Leave for twenty-four hours in a warm place. Open the mould and trim away any surplus latex from the join, and cut off the end of the neck with a sharp knife.

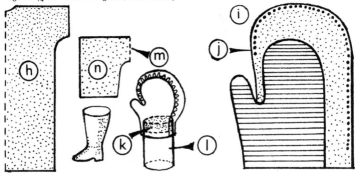

Fig. 17 (¼ in.=1 in. For glove, actual size)

BOXERS

Materials and Tools These must be selected according to method. The Boxers can be made with papier mâché or latex (moulding rubber) heads; the boxing gloves made from scraps of leather, or modelled and cast and made in latex or moulding rubber too. Cut the puppet glove as in fig. 17(h). Stitch up sides and shoulder seams, hem the bottom. Stick the head into the neck hole with contact adhesive (cement). For the boxing gloves cut two soft pieces of leather for each hand (i). The shaded area is for the palm, the dotted area plus the shaded area for the back. The pattern is actual size. Run a thread round the outside of the back (j), gathering it so that it fits round the palm. Over-sew the two parts together. If shellac is available use a little to stiffen the palm. Make a cardboard finger tube and glue to the glove (l), stuff some bran, kapok or foam rubber into the glove so that it holds its shape. Shave a cork to the right size and glue into the wrist to hold the stuffing in place (k). Now glue the arms into the glove. Smear carpet thread with glue and twist several times round each wrist and tie, fig. 16(f).

Fig. 16(g) shows the addition of legs; these can be made in latex (moulding rubber), papier mâché, or shaped with a sharp knife from two corks stuck together to make the appropriate shape. Cut two pieces for the trousers as fig. 17(n), placing the dotted line on a fold (m). Sew up sides and crotch seams. Insert a little stuffing. Glue the legs into the trouser legs and stitch the top of the trousers to the inside front of the glove. The operator's hand can slip into the glove and the legs dangle in front of the wrist. Should latex or moulding rubber be used, paint with special rubber paint or acrylic paints. Paint papier mâché with poster colours or emulsion paint. If using poster colours it is advisable to varnish them.

3 Rod puppets

After some experience of glove or hand puppets, most people are ready to experiment with something which will give more scope for variation of action. The obvious step is to try rod puppets. Until very recently these have been much more popular in far eastern countries than in Europe, where the tradition of the Punch and Judy show has died hard. Many of the rod puppets from Java are very beautiful indeed, with elegant heads and long thin arms, sometimes dressed in decorative printed cotton, sometimes in thin silk decorated with tiny sequins (see page 35).

An example of the extensive use of rod puppets today is the Soviet Central Puppet Theatre with its wide repertoire of plays for both juvenile and adult audiences. To see these puppets in action will convince the spectator of the vast possibilities of work with rod puppets.

When creating rod puppets it is essential to bear in mind that it is in their arm and head actions that they excel, so it is well worth becoming skilled in either modelling or carving expressive hands and heads if plays are going to be produced in this way. There are many ways of concealing the action rods: the main holding rod is usually hidden by the robe or tunic of the puppet, or under one trouser leg if the figure has been designed with legs; the action rods are usually connected with the hands, and are either thin dowel or metal rods. Hanging sleeves or a cloak cleverly draped can enfold the rods, or the hand can be holding a staff, a broomstick or a parasol.

In elaborate productions it may be necessary to make several identical figures which are constructed to perform different movements; with a complicated puppet two people may be needed to manipulate it. It is essential however to master very basic puppets first, which are made to perform very simple actions. A short scene sensitively performed between two operators, each working with one puppet, will be the best way to start, and a third person sitting in front giving guidance and sensible criticism will be a great help.

Instructions follow for a variety of rod puppets, and much of the advice given in one example could well be helpful in any of the other figures, and by looking through the drawings it will be obvious how different limbs, etc, could be interchangeable. The use of plastic tubing for arms as described in the string marionette section can also be referred to (page 52).

A very simple rod puppet

Materials Plastic yogurt pot (or similar size); ping-pong ball; length of dowel; carpet thread; cardboard; contact adhesive (cement); feathers and trimmings; cotton material; sewing thread; coloured inks.

Tools Needles and pins; awl; scissors; ruler; pencil.

Following fig. 18, place the dress pattern on the material with (a)–(b) on a fold. Cut two pieces, following the starred cutting line. Sew up the side seam but leave the neck and bottom open. Notch as indicated at (d). Heat the point of an awl in a flame and make holes in the ping-pong ball (e) to take the rod and the plug of dowel for the nose (f). In the yogurt pot (g) make a large hole (h). Insert the length of dowel (i) in the ping-pong ball, fixing with contact adhesive (cement), fig. 19(j). Fix the bottom of the dress (b)–(c) to the bottom of the pot with contact adhesive (cement) (l). Thread the rod through the neck of the dress and then through the hole in the pot. Fix the dress to the rod at the neck with a dab of contact adhesive (cement), and for extra strength tie with a length of carpet thread (k). Strands of wool (yarn) or silk thread may be stuck in place for hair (o). Cut a ring of cardboard, making tabs in the middle (m), and glue this to the ping-pong ball to form the brim of the hat.

Fig. 18 ($\frac{1}{4}$ in.=1 in.)

Fig. 19

Paint the top of the ping-pong ball the same colour as the hat brim so that it looks like the crown of the hat. The trimming can be of tiny artificial flowers or small pieces of feather and scraps of net. If the result needs a little stiffening, a puff from an aerosol hair spray will do the trick. A small piece of lace or frilled edging can be stuck round the neck to look like a collar or, alternatively, some feather trimming or a length of gathered net will look like an old-fashioned feather boa. A little light weight shawl and an apron would give character.

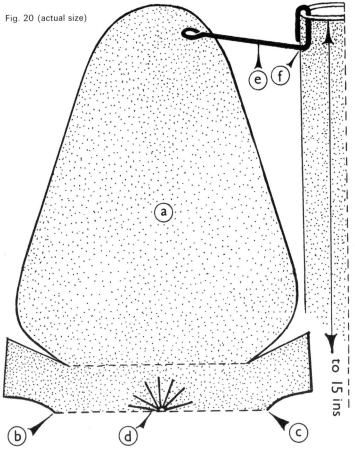

Fig. 20 (actual size)

(a)

(b) (d) (c)

(e) (f)

to 15 ins

Basic rod puppet

Materials 15 in. of cardboard tube, 1 in. diameter; 20 in. wooden dowel rod, ⅝ in. diameter; wire; thin cardboard; gumstrip (gummed tape); newspaper; modelling clay or plasticine; cold water paste; thin foam rubber sheet (optional); beads (optional); poster or other suitable paints; thin wood or metal rods; materials for dressing.

Tools Ruler; scissors; pencil; small saw or Stanley knife; pliers with cutting edge; paste brush; paint brushes; some kind of modelling tool.

The construction given here is for a basic rod puppet which can very easily be adapted to a variety of characters of many different sizes and shapes. This can be done by adding to the construction with pieces of thin foam rubber glued in place with a contact adhesive (cement), or by varying the basic cardboard shape, or by the addition of further papier mâché.

First take the dowel rod (fig. 21q) and model a head on to the end of it. If a loosely-crumpled ball of newspaper is fixed to the top of the rod with wire (r), clay or plasticine may be modelled over the top; this uses less modelling substance and also makes the head lighter. Paste several layers of torn-up newspaper on to the head with cold water paste and leave to dry.

Cut the body shape from thin cardboard, (fig. 20) (a), with (b)-(c) the centre line; make radiating cuts at the centre (d). Make the shoulder wires from two $2\frac{1}{2}$ in. lengths of wire which are passed through holes made in the cardboard tube (f), and bent firmly into position as (e). Shape the body by scoring along the shoulder line and overlapping the flaps, securing them in place with gum-strip (gummed tape), fig. 21 (g). Place the body in position on the tube and fix with more gumstrip (h); also join the sides together in a similar way (i). Now paste several layers of torn scraps of newspaper all over the body to make a nice firm papier mâché shape, paying particular attention to the neck and shoulder line as this must form a firm foundation on which the neck will rest, (j). Cut the arm wires, making loops top and bottom of the upper arm. Strips of newspaper soaked in cold water paste can be wound round the wires to build up the shape of the arms (k) or wooden beads can be threaded on to the wires (l). The wire for the lower arm is threaded into a hand cut from the cardboard (m) and then given a coating of small scraps of newspaper. Inter-link wires at the shoulders and elbows (n) and (o) after the arms are quite dry. Either one or two hand operating rods made of thin dowel or metal rod can be fixed to the hands with thin wire and a dab of contact adhesive (cement) (s). A thin layer of foam rubber glued on to the firm papier mâché body shape will be helpful in fixing the costume on to the puppet.

Now insert the dowel rod with the head into the neck of the body. Bind thin string or wire firmly round the rod making a thick collar (p) which prevents the head from dropping too far into the shoulders. Coat this with glue. When dry, the puppet is ready for dressing and painting.

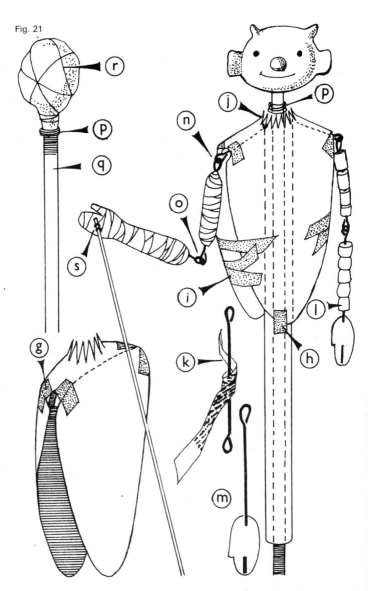

Fig. 21

Fig. 22 (½ in.=1 in.)

Ghost: an extending rod puppet

Extending puppets are traditional.
Materials Newspaper; polythene
(polyethylene) bag; wire; dowel;
hair curlers; two plastic pots the
size of yogurt pots; carpet and
button hole thread; sewing thread;
thin cotton material; 3 in. wood
1 in.×¼ in.; paints; glue; cold
water paste; two beads.
Tools Scissors; pliers; pins;
needles; ruler; drill; paint brush;
small saw, knife or chisel.
Following fig. 22 make the shoulder
bar, from 1 in.×¼ in. wood (a). Saw
off corners and sandpaper. Drill a
large hole to take the dowel (b),
and two small holes to take the
shoulder threads (c); through
these holes tie loops of thread
to link with the hair curlers (e).
Carve bone-like forearms from
dowel (f), drill a hole through
the top (g) and into the wrist
(h). Glue each bead into a
curler, thread carpet thread
through bead and arm (g) and tie
(d). Make armatures of wire for
the hands (i), round these twist
strips of torn newspaper soaked
in cold water paste until the
hand (j) is built up. Glue the
hand to the wrist (h). Take two
plastic pots (k) and drill holes in
them to take the dowel (l).
Glue the shoulder bar 2 in. from
the top of the rod, with the
arms in place. Next glue one of
the yogurt pots 1 in. lower down,
fig. 23(t). Leave to dry.
Cut two pieces for the robe (m),
placing the dotted line on a fold.
N.B. extend the pattern until it

Fig. 23

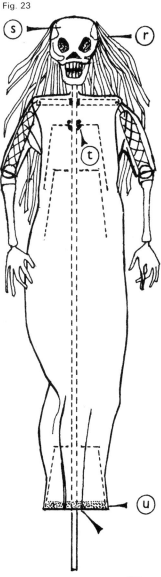

37

Fig. 24

Fig. 25

measures 15 in. Notch as shown (n). Sew up shoulder and under arm seams, with the dowel protruding through the neck hole. Make a head from papier mâché fig. 23(s), following the method on page 24. Make a hole to take the rod and fix with contact adhesive (cement). Thread the second pot on to the rod and glue the bottom to the skirt (u). The pot now slides up and down the rod altering the height of the puppet. Strips of polythene (polyethylene) make the hair; the hat, cut as fig. 22(q), can now be glued to the head, and the puppet is ready for painting.

If the addition of legs is desirable fig. 25 shows how this may be done. The drawings are not to scale. Cut feet from pieces of balsa wood (v). Before threading the lower plastic pot on to the rod, make two holes in the pot with a hot awl as (y) and a set of holes down one side (z). Take 12 in. of wire and thread through holes (y) and bend slightly at the bottom, push these ends into the balsa wood feet as (x), and glue. Paste strips of papier mâché over the feet and bind round the legs until they are thick enough (z1). With the awl, burn away a little of the lip of the pot below the holes. Using a needle and button hole thread, tie the stick to the pot and then spread glue at these points. Paint the feet and legs, thread the pot onto the rod, and then glue the skirt to the bottom of the pot as previously described.

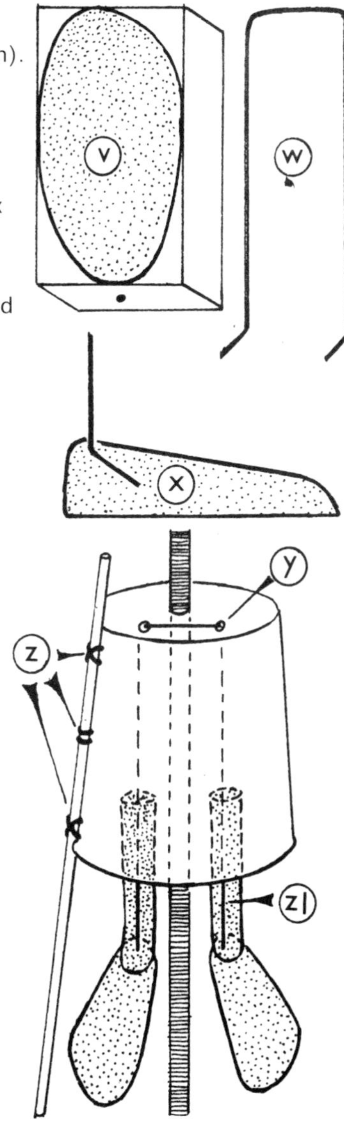

Fig. 26 ($\frac{1}{2}$ in.=1 in.)

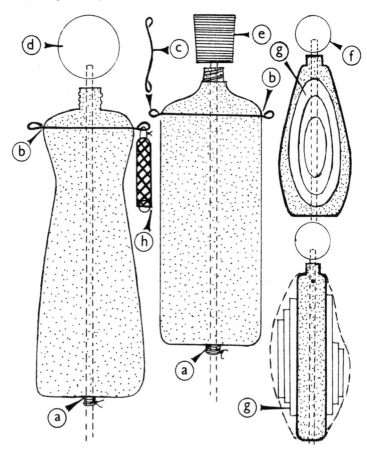

Rod puppets from plastic bottles

Materials Plastic bottles of various shapes; corks or ping-pong balls for heads; wire; hair curlers and balsa wood for arms; dowel; screw eyes; carpet thread; thin sheet foam rubber for padding; paints, fabrics etc. for costuming; contact adhesive (cement). *Tools* Pliers; awl; scissors; ruler; Stanley knife; sandpaper.

Plastic bottles come in many shapes and sizes and these make satisfactory puppets. The bottle may suggest a suitable character, but sometimes it needs improvement and the shape can often be adjusted by the addition of padding made of thin foam rubber cut to shape and built up in layers, as in fig. 26 (g).

Holes which are needed to take rods or wires should be made with the point of an awl heated in a flame. One hole should be made in the base of the bottle to take the rod, and one hole on each side of the shoulders for the cross bar which holds the arms, (b). Push a length of wire into one armhole and out through the other; then, with a pair of pointed-nosed pliers or a screwdriver, press the centre of the wire so that it takes a slight curve (c). This prevents it from touching the centre rod. Using the pliers, make a loop at each side (b). If curlers are being used for arms, tie these through the loops with thread.

Put the dowel through the base of the puppet and push it up far enough to make the neck of the puppet plus $\frac{3}{4}$ inch. Wind some carpet thread round the dowel and smear it with glue (a), so that the bottle is held in place.

Make a hole in the ping-pong ball or cork (d), (e), (f) and glue in place on top of the dowel for the head. Thread bound under the head and dabbed with glue will make it more secure.

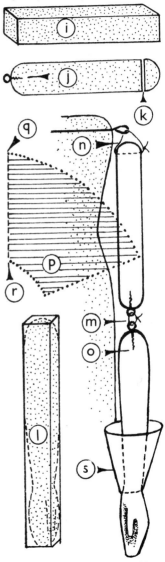

Fig. 27 (actual size)

41

The square bottle suggests the character of a soldier. Fig. 27 shows how the arms are made from balsa wood. Cut two lengths (i) suitably proportioned to the bottle, and using a sharp blade or knife, shave the wood into shape. Into one end insert a small screw eye (j), through the other end make a hole with an awl (k). From the second length of wood cut a forearm and hand, (l), fixing another screw eye at the elbow. Join the two screw eyes loosely with carpet thread and dab the knot with glue (m), and then join the upper arm to shoulder loop in the same way (n). From white PVC (sheet plastic) or cardboard cut two gauntlet shapes (p) for the gloves, placing (q–r) on a fold (s). Use black PVC (sheet plastic) or felt to cover the bottle body; first wrap round the bottle making holes for the shoulder loops, and glue at the back, then nick the top into tabs and glue them down one at a time until the shoulder is covered neatly, fig. 28(t). Cut the collar (u) with dotted line on a fold, and stick in place. Draw the epaulettes from pattern (v), fringing the edge with scissors (w). Stick thin wire down the centre (x), leave to dry. Bend to shape, testing that they do not hinder the arm action. Fix in place and finish with a plastic-headed pin (y). Paint the cork head, sticking in knobbed pins for eyes; make a military moustache from bristles or plastic raffia, by tying in the middle, stick with contact glue (cement). The soldier in the drawing has a hat made from a gilt whiskey bottle stopper, to which a scrap of ostrich feather has been glued; other caps and stoppers could be used for differently-shaped hats. Paint hands to match the gauntlets and arms to match tunic, trim the tunic with paper braid and small beads, buttons or sequins. Fix an action wire to the saluting hand (z).

The waisted bottled at left of fig. 26 suggests a Victorian shape and fig. 29 shows how it can be easily transformed into an elegant Bo-peep. Each arm is made from two white curlers which look like net sleeves. The puppet is entirely dressed from one soft plastic dressing table mat. Cut a straight piece of the required length, using the scalloped edge for the bottom of the dress. Smear the waist with Bostik, Elmer's glue or Sobo and make some little tucks at the centre front and back, then glue the centre back seam and stick it together. Trim and glue the plastic material so that it fits the shoulders, tie a ribbon round the waist. Cut a large circle from the remaining material and run a gathering thread round the edge, draw up to fit the head and stick in place. Cut suitably shaped pieces of edging to make a frilly edge. Bend a piece of cane in steam to make the crook.

The third bottle in fig. 26 becomes Old King Cole, as in fig. 30.

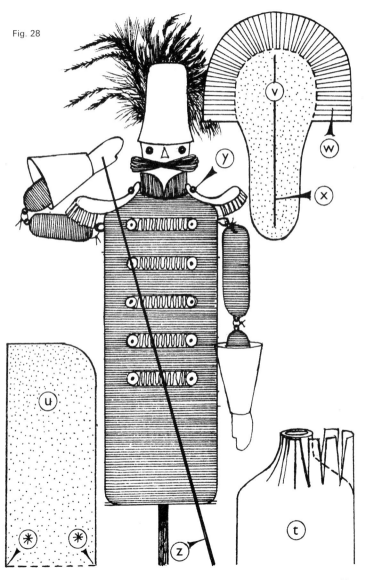

Fig. 28

43

Fig. 29

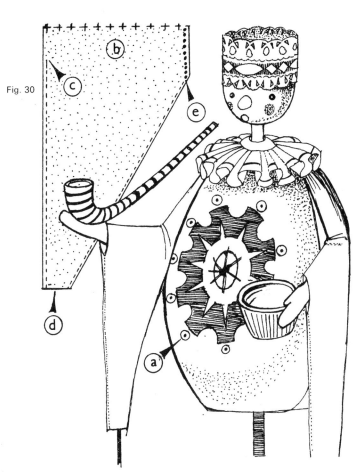

Fig. 30

Soak thin, loose-weave cotton in cold water paste and stretch it across the padded shape (this will need to be done in two pieces) and allow to dry. Then give them a coat of paint. Decorate with cut felt and sequins (a). Cut 2 sleeves as pattern (b) placing crosses on fold; these should be of very soft material such as jap (China) silk. Partially join the seams, leaving open at (c) for hand and (d) for arm wire. Seams will have to be completed after sleeves are in position or it will be impossible to pass them over hands and wires. Run a gathering thread round the armhole (e), draw up and tie so that the sleeve is held in position. Make a ruff from frilled edging and stitch round neck. Paint the ping-pong ball head and add a crown of gold paper lace from a cake frill.

4 Marionettes: puppets with strings

Whereas glove (hand) and rod puppets are operated from below, marionettes are operated from above, and when used in conjunction with a theatre the manipulator needs to stand on a platform or *bridge* as it is called. However, quite a lot of fun can be had from operating the puppets without a theatre, in the manner of a professional puppeteer who works them in a cabaret. Although many marionettes are difficult to make and manipulate, great joy can be had by children using simpler forms. It is essential that very simple stringing should be used, otherwise the operation will end in tangles and temper.

In this section a number of different methods of construction are given so that craftsmen of various capabilities and interests can have an opportunity to experiment. The general idea that string puppets involve the use of carpentry tools to a fairly high standard prevents many people from setting to work. Consequently various ways of building up puppets by making sewn shapes, or by using such materials as may be easily cut with a Stanley knife or good penknife, are described. A principle to be remembered is that marionettes are easier to manipulate if they are not too light; the weight should be concentrated in the lower limbs so that the movement of the feet can be satisfactorily sensed.

However adept the manipulator, the minimum of strings required for movements should be used – a cluttered control is merely an encumbrance. As in designing other forms of puppets, the actions the marionette is to make must be considered from the outset and the figure built around them, so that the operator controls the marionette's movements instead of being inhibited by the actions it is eventually found capable of performing. It is vital to remember that the marionette is not just a little person in the hands of a giant.

Simple stuffed puppets

The very simple examples shown in fig. 31 can be made by young children. Oblongs of material are cut and stitched into small bags, which are stuffed with kapok, bran or foam rubber crumbs. The bags are then sewn up and over-sewn together. Strings attached to the shoulders (a) and to one leg (b) are tied to a holding stick (c). From the head tie a length of black hat elastic which, when pulled downwards, will give a nodding action (d). Inventive use of materials will create amusing puppets, and extra details can be added as shown in the little character with hair of looped rug wool (yarn) (e).

46

Fig. 31

Fig. 32 ($\frac{1}{4}$ in.=1 in.)

HARLEQUIN AND COLUMBINE

These can be made with either papier mâché or latex (moulding rubber) heads, as described on pages 24 and 26. Tools and materials should be chosen accordingly.

Materials for the Harlequin
A stocking; felt; PVC (sheet plastic); sewing thread; frilled edging; 5 in. of dowel; round elastic; carpet thread; latex (rubber-based) glue.
Tools Scissors; needles; pins; ruler; pencil.

Following fig. 32 (a), cut a piece from a stocking 18 in. long and sew to make the legs before cutting the line (b) to separate them. Turn the stocking inside out and stuff as far as the knees, then make two stitching lines (c). Stuff to the top of the legs, and stitch again (d). Now stuff to the waist and make two lines of stitching (e). Continue with the stuffing until the neck is almost reached, then over-sew the shoulder seams (f) and (g), before putting in the last bit of stuffing. Glue the neck of the previously made head (h) into the stocking neck. Make the arms by cutting two pieces (i), placing the pattern on a fold. Sew up and stuff, sew the top and draw up the thread (j), fix to the shoulders. The puppet is now ready for dressing.

Cut the hat from either PVC (sheet plastic) or felt, cutting

Fig. 33

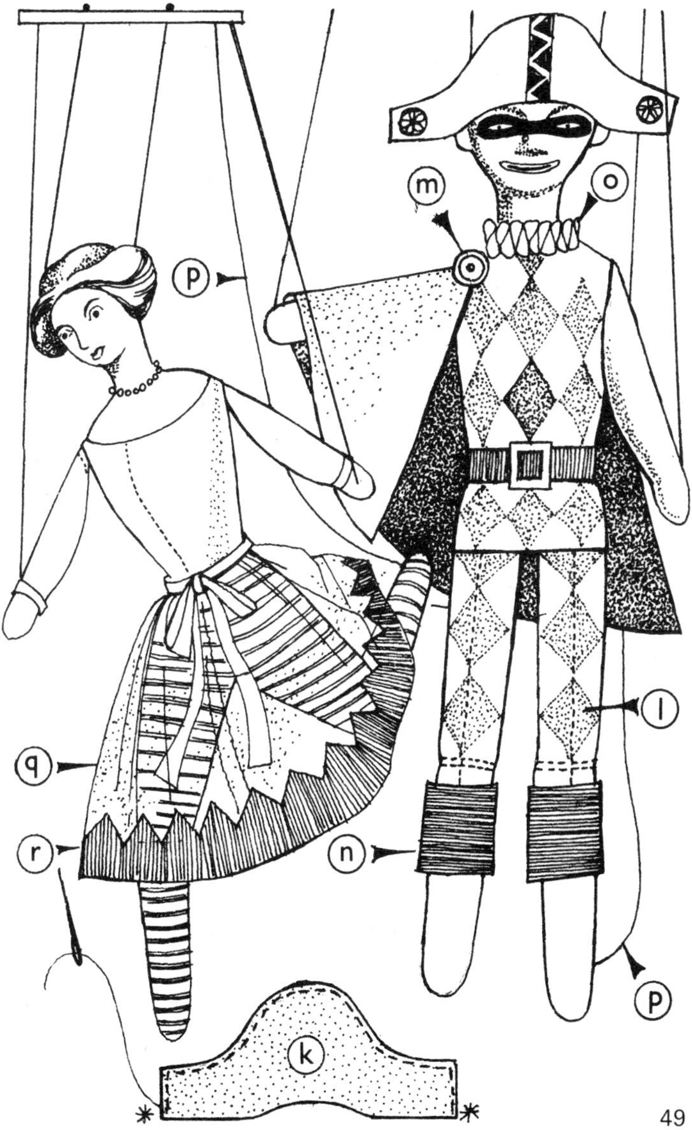

49

Fig. 34 ($\frac{1}{4}$ in.=1 in.)

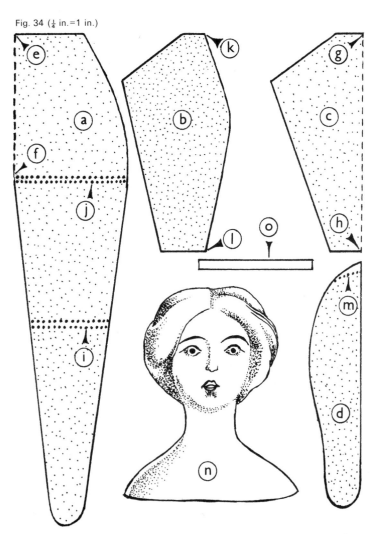

two pieces as fig. 33(k). Sew as indicated and add trimmings, then glue in position with latex (rubber-based) adhesive. Cut some diamonds from felt as (l) and stick in place. A felt cloak is sewn to the shoulders with a decorative button (m). A length of frilled edging or a ruffle is fixed about the neck. Make cuffs from PVC (sheet plastic) to simulate the tops of boots and glue into position (n). A PVC (sheet plastic) belt can be made and trimmed with a small buckle.

The Columbine (based on the Victorian puppet shown on page 71.) First make a head and neck base as fig. 34(n) in latex (moulding rubber) or papier mâché. The arms and legs of the puppet are made from cotton material, and the bodice from a small piece of velvet. Cut two pieces for the legs as fig. 34(a), placing (e)–(f) on a fold (striped material is effective for this). Cut two double pieces as (d) for the arms; for the body, cut two pieces as (b) for the front, and one piece as (c) with (g)–(h) on a fold for the back. First sew together the centre front seam of the bodice (k)–(l). Next sew the front of the bodice to the back leaving only the waist seam open. Sew up the arms leaving open at (m). Stitch the legs, leaving open at the waist. Turn all the pieces right side out. Begin by stuffing the legs through the waist opening as far as the knee joint, and then make two lines of stitching (i). Continue to the tops of the legs and stitch again (j), fill to the top and over-sew the waist. Stuff the bodice and over-sew the waist, then over-sew the bodice and legs together. Stuff the arms up to (m), make a line of stitching and finally over-sew the top of the arm; this leaves a small flange of unstuffed material which makes the arm more mobile. Stitch the arm in position. Glue the inside of the neck base with contact adhesive (cement) and press firmly to the top of the velvet bodice. Leave to dry. Make a gauzy skirt; book muslin looks well and is cheap. In fig. 33 it is shown with an edging of silver beadec. Bangles are made of silver ribbon, and a ribbon is tied loosely round the waist.

Both puppets have similar stringing. Thread a carpet needle with a length of round elastic and pass through the head, fix each end to a holding bar of dowel; the elastic can be tied to the bar or passed through drilled holes and tied to wooden beads. Use carpet thread for arm and leg strings, experimenting to find what length is best for movement. In fig. 33 the leg string on each puppet is marked (p). When the puppet is gently bounced there is secondary movement due to the interaction between the stretchy elastic and the taut carpet thread; in addition the arm and leg strings can be manipulated with the right hand whilst the left hand is holding the bar.

A VERY EASY MARIONETTE USING PLASTIC TUBING

The completed puppet is illustrated on page 58.

Materials Calico; bran or shavings; plastic tubing $\frac{1}{2}$ in. and $\frac{3}{4}$ in. diameter; plastic or wooden ball 2 in. diameter; tape; cardboard; carpet thread; sewing thread; curtain ring; screw eyes; contact adhesive (cement).

Tools Awl; needles and pins; ruler; sharp blade or knife; knitting needle.

Following fig. 35, first make the body by cutting two pieces of calico as (a), no seam allowance shown. Sew up sides and bottom but leave (b)–(c) open. Turn right side out and stuff with either bran or shavings. While over-sewing the shoulder seams, insert a 1 in. curtain ring so that half of it protrudes above the shoulder line in the neck position.

Now cut the tubing for the arms and legs. If the tubing needs straightening, this can be done by dipping it into boiling water and bending it to shape, and then dipping it into cold water. For the legs, use $\frac{3}{4}$ in. diameter tube and cut two pieces 4 in. long (e) and (g), and two pieces $3\frac{1}{2}$ in. long (i) and (k); for the arms, using the $\frac{1}{2}$ in. tubing, cut two pieces $3\frac{1}{2}$ in. long (s) and two pieces 3 in. long (u).

Before proceeding any further look carefully at the details (o), (p) and (n); (n) is the section of tube when a right-angled cut has been made, (p) shows how it should be cleanly sliced with a knife at a forty-five-degree angle to arrive at (o). Beginning with the upper part of the leg, following (i) which shows the side view, cut away two sections (j) and (m); then, as shown in the front view (k), make two small holes with the heated point of an awl (l). Next prepare the lower part of the leg: following (e) which is the side view, cut off a section (f). Then, as front view (g), make a small hole (h) as before; into this hole twist and glue a screw eye.

The side section of the upper arm (s) indicates where a section (t) must be cut away. The front view (q) shows the position of a small hole (r). The lower arm (u) should have a 1 in. slit made in it, this can then be nicked and the lower part of the tube opened out (hot and cold water will help) to form a hand, (w). Cut two pieces of stiff cardboard (z) for the soles of the feet, and find a ball 2 in. in diameter for the head. This can be a wooden ball from a timber shop or a vinyl (plastic) ball from a toy shop. Apart from the control the pieces are now ready for assembly.

Fig. 35 ($\frac{1}{2}$ in.=1 in.)

Fig. 36

Now look at fig. 36. First put the arms together following (b). Take some ordinary tape and thread it through the two sections gluing at X with contact adhesive (cement); a knitting needle pushed into the tube will press the tape in place. Stitch the top end of the tape securely to the shoulder (c). Cut a piece of tape to join the legs at the knee joint, and glue this firmly inside the tubes above and below the joint as (e), taking care not to get any glue into the joint itself. Make a tiny hole in the upper part of the knee joint and glue a small screw eye into it (f). Sew the legs to the body with carpet thread, through the holes already prepared (g).

To attach the head, pierce the wooden ball with an awl and then fix a screw eye into the hole (d), open the screw eye slightly with pliers and ease the curtain ring neck (a) on to it, then close up the screw eye so that the head and neck are linked. If a vinyl ball is used a wire must be put straight through it as shown in fig. 35(y) and this is looped through the curtain ring and then tightly closed. A second wire (y1) makes loops to take the head strings. The feet can be built up with papier mâché as shown in fig. 36(i), after gluing the cardboard soles on to the ends of the legs. Strengthen the hand by gluing a wire in place (h).

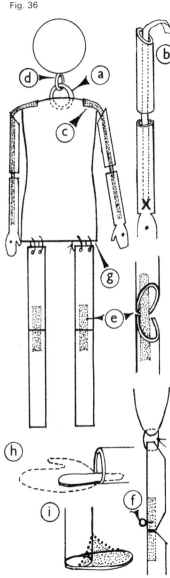

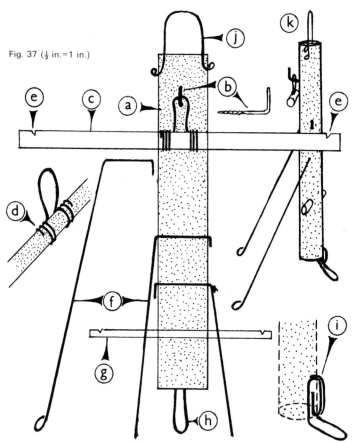

Fig. 37 (½ in.=1 in.)

Fig. 37 shows the control used for this kind of marionette. First cut 7 in. of 1 in. diameter cardboard tube (a). Make a hole to take a large cup hook (b) or a stout bent wire and push this through the tube about one inch from the top, glue contact points. This takes the leg bar (c), a 7 in. length of $\frac{5}{16}$ in. dowel: make a wire loop round the centre of the bar (d) so that it will hang on the hook. Notch each end of the bar (e). Make holes through the tube with a sharp awl for the arm wires (f); these should be bent into loops at the ends to take strings. Make large holes to take 4 in. of $\frac{3}{16}$ in. dowel (g) for the head strings. A bowing string (h), to make the puppet bow, can be added by bending double a 3 in. length of wire and pushing it through a hole 1 in. from the base of the tube; starting from the inside, bend the cut ends round the bottom

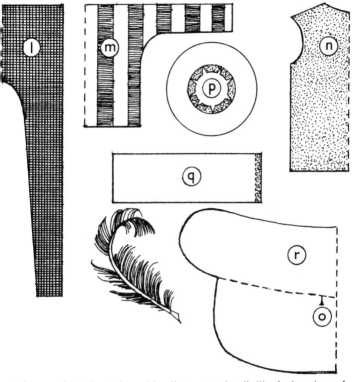

Fig. 38 ($\frac{1}{4}$ in.=1 in.)

and press into the tube with pliers, see detail (i). A drawing of the side view of the control is shown at (k). In order to be able to hang the puppet when not in use make two holes about 1 in. from the top of the tube, push a 2 in. wire through the holes and make a loop as shown (j).

The puppet should be dressed before it is ready to be strung. Use soft cotton for the trousers and shirt; a thin knitted material such as stockinette would do well. Cut 2 pieces each, as in fig. 38 (l) and (m) for the trousers and shirt, placing the dotted line on a fold, allow $\frac{1}{4}$ in. for turnings. Sew up trouser seams, stitch on to puppet at waist; sew side seams of shirt, put on puppet and then sew shoulder seams. For the waistcoat, cut one piece (n) with dotted line on a fold for the back, and 2 single pieces for fronts.

Fig. 39

Stitch and fit. Felt would be a suitable material. Cut the hat from felt; (p) is the brim and (q) the crown. Trim with a feather. The half collar pattern is drawn full size; cut from white felt, score and fold on the dotted line (o), and glue or sew round neck. Some strands of tow (flax or hemp) or rug wool (yarn) make the hair.

To string the puppet use no. 18 carpet thread. Begin with the head. The length of the strings depends on the height of the operator and the position of working. Tie the head strings to the wires at the side of the head and to the notches in the head bar while the puppet is lying on the floor. The strings must be equal in length. Then do the same with the legs, tying the strings to the screw eyes in the knees and the notches on the leg bar, and leaving enough slack to enable the bar to be lifted from the control without affecting the legs. Hang the puppet up and stitch a string to the centre back of the hip; tie this to the bowing loop, again allowing some slackness. Pierce the hands and thread a string with a knot on the end through the hole, tie the other end through the loops at the ends of the arm wires. It is best if the lengths of the arm strings are slightly different and one of the arms is very slightly raised. Touch all knots with glue to keep them secure.

Fig. 40

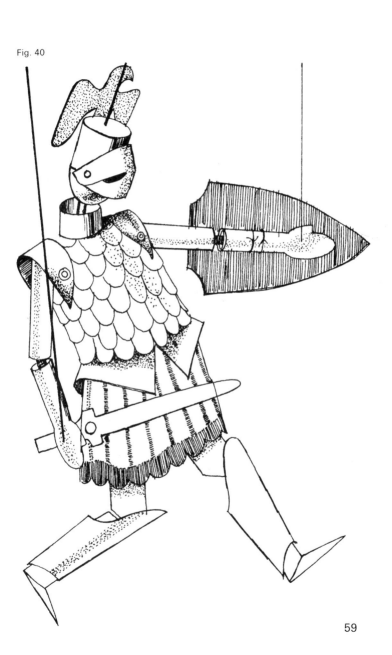

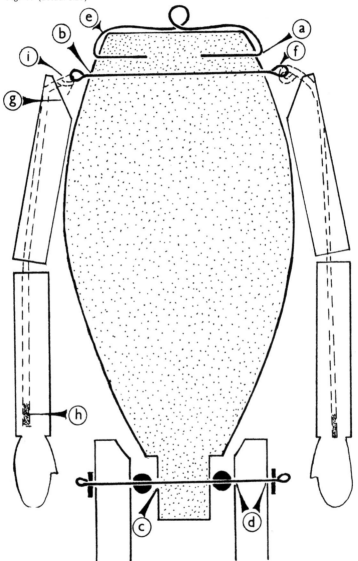

Fig. 41 (actual size)

60

Fig. 42

KNIGHT IN ARMOUR

This is based on a Sicilian marionette (see page 54).

Materials Plastic bottle; plastic tubing; tape; wire; wooden beads; washers; paper fasteners; carpet thread; 1½ in. diameter wooden ball; gold paper and cardboard; scrap of shirting; Bostik, Elmer's glue or Sobo.
Tools Scissors; ruler; pliers; Stanley knife; awl; drill.

First make the necessary holes in the bottle (fig. 41) with the heated point of an awl; 2 holes (a) for the neck loop, 2 holes (b) for the arm bar, and 2 holes (c) for the leg wire. Cut wire and form the neck loop as (e). Then cut a wire and push through the arm holes, making small loops at each end (f). Cut pieces of ⅜ in. diameter plastic tubing with a Stanley knife for the arms; the upper arm should be 2 in. long and the lower arm 2½ in. long. Pare off a small section (g) to avoid tangling the wire loop. Thread a length of tape through the tubing, glue at the wrist (h) and stitch round the wire loop at the top (i). For the legs follow fig. 42. Cut two lengths of plastic tubing 3½ in. long for the top of the leg; (j) shows a front view. Pare away a small piece at the top so that the top of the leg does not hit the body (k). Also cut away a section from the back of the knee joint (l) (side view).

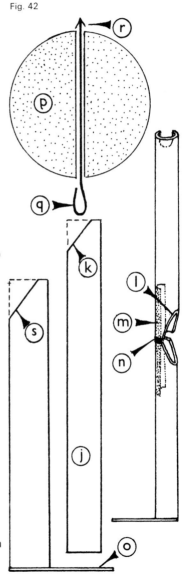

61

Fig. 43

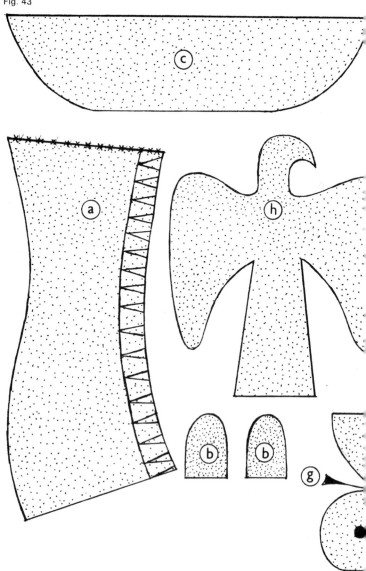

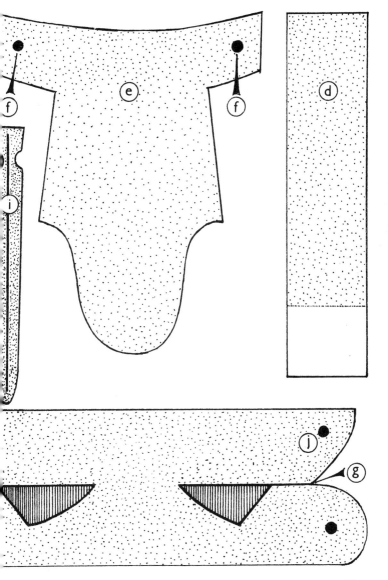

63

Cut 2 pieces 3 in. long for the lower leg, again cutting away a section of the back of the knee (s). Glue a piece of tape inside the tubing to join the two leg sections (m) taking care that the tape at the joint (n) does not become congealed with the glue. Cut out a cardboard foot and stick to the base of the lower leg (o).

Turn back to fig. 41 to see how the legs should be joined to the body. First make holes with a hot awl through the plastic tubing at the tops of the legs (d). Make a small loop at the end of a length of wire, thread on a small washer, then push the wire through the holes at (d), thread a small wooden bead on the wire; now push the wire through the holes previously made in the bottle at (c). Repeat in reverse and finish off by making another small wire loop – do not tighten the wire too much.

Take the wooden ball (p), drill a hole through it as in fig. 42, and pass a length of wire through, making a good-sized loop at the neck end (q) which must be linked with the neck loop previously made on the bottle. The wire protruding from the top of the head (r) is an action wire and should be cut off at a convenient length (say 12 in.) for operation. If a drill is not available, put screw eyes into the head – link the neck one with the neck loop, and link a 12 in. wire tightly through the one at the top of the head. The puppet is now ready for dressing.

First make a basic breastplate shape by slightly padding the front of the bottle with some plastic foam sheeting, 2 or 3 thin layers on the front and slightly less on the back are all that will be necessary. Over this stretch and glue some net to make a firm shape. Make a skirt from a small piece of shirting; it should be very slightly gathered and reach almost to the knees. It can be glued in place. Following fig. 43, cut 2 pieces (a) of gold-surfaced card; these form the bottom of the breastplate. The crosses show the centre front. Cut tabs as indicated and bend along the inner line. Glue in place above the skirt (see fig. 40). Then build up the rest of the breastplate with scales cut from gold paper (b), starting at the bottom and overlapping them until the body is covered. Cut two shoulder pieces (c) and glue into place. Cut one piece for the neck gorget (d) and fix round the neck. Cut two greaves (shin plates) as (e). Smear the front of the shin with glue and stick the greave in place, when dry link points marked (f) with a paper fastener. Cut a piece (j) for the visor of the helmet, cutting along the lines (g) and cutting away the darkly shaded areas. Following fig. 44 cut the top of the helmet (l) and the side (k), bend the latter into a tube and glue, bend the tabs of (l) and glue inside the tube. Take the visor and

Fig. 44 (for l and k ½ in.=1 in.)

overlap the dark spots on each side, push a gilt paper fastener through and into the sides of the helmet and fix. Stick the eagle, fig. 43(h), in place at the back. Thread the helmet over the head wire and turn over the end of the wire to make a loop or hook as fig. 44(m). Cut a shield from the cardboard (see fig. 40), pierce and tie to the arm, adding a little glue to make it secure. The pattern for the sword is shown in fig. 43(i); cut 2 thicknesses and glue together with a length of wire between them. Tie and glue this into the right hand. A length of wire, which should be longer than the head wire, is then glued into a hole made in the wrist. Bend the wire at the top into a hook as in fig. 44(o) so that it can hang over the head loop when the puppet is not in use. For the shield arm use string (n); the kind used in the original marionette is quite thick and looks better in proportion to the wire than carpet thread.

The actions made by this marionette are primitive but they have character and verve, and with a little practice it will be found that the figure can be manipulated into many positions simply by swinging it.

Fig. 45 ($\frac{1}{2}$ in.=1 in.)

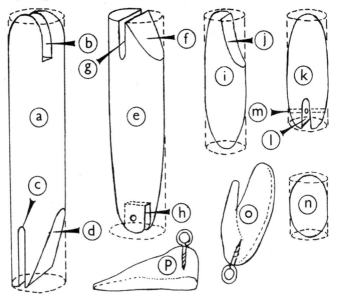

An advanced marionette

The most satisfactory kind of marionette for use over a long period of time is one made mostly from wood. This will stand up to a lot of wear and tear, will not deteriorate if it is left hanging up unused, and can be packed and unpacked from a skip (wicker basket) or suitcase and be none the worse for it.

To construct one of these marionettes you need to be familiar with the use of carpentry tools, and to be able to make neat accurate saw cuts and to be adept with a chisel. These are accomplishments that the craftsman can acquire with a little practice. Patience is also required, as this kind of marionette is not made in a few hours.

Materials Dowel rod 1$\frac{1}{2}$ in. and $\frac{3}{4}$ in. diameter; one 2$\frac{1}{2}$ in. diameter wooden ball; wire; screw eyes; small pieces of leather; Bostik (Elmer's glue or Sobo) and Seccotine (Duco Cement); carpet thread; suitable off-cuts of wood for the body; paints and fabrics for dressing and trimming.

Tools Small sharp saw; awl; pliers; chisels (say 1 in., $\frac{1}{2}$ in. and $\frac{1}{8}$ in. widths); ruler; scissors; drill.

Referring to fig. 45, first cut the necessary lengths of $1\frac{1}{2}$ in. dowel for the legs, and $\frac{3}{4}$ in. dowel for the arms. For the upper leg (a) round off the top with a chisel and then cut the slot (b) by first making two clean saw cuts and then clearing the wood away with the $\frac{1}{8}$ in. chisel. This slot should be the right width to take a double thickness of the leather which is being used for the hinge joints. Now cut the slot (c) to take a single thickness of leather for the upper part of the knee joint. Next saw a slice from the dowel to give the angle (d), which allows the knee to bend. For the lower leg (e), round off the lower end of the dowel and then cut the slot (h) forming the ankle; this should be wide enough to take the head of a screw eye and allow it to move freely backwards and forwards. Cut the groove (g) to take one thickness of leather, and cut away the back to complete the knee joint (f).

The upper arm (i) and the forearm (k) are cut from the $\frac{3}{4}$ in. dowel. Round off the top and bottom of (i) and then with a chisel cut away the wood at the top to get section (j); this helps the arm to lie against the body. Insert a screw eye at each end of the limb. Round off the top and bottom of the forearm (k) and cut a slot (l) wide enough to take the top of a screw eye, also drill a hole to take the sawn-off shaft of the nail (m).

Cut a length of $\frac{3}{4}$ in. dowelling for the neck, round off the two ends (n) and insert screw eyes both top and bottom. When inserting screw eyes, first make a small hole with an awl as this helps to prevent the wood from splitting, also dip the screw end into a spot of Seccotine (Duco Cement) before screwing it home as this gives extra security. From small pieces of wood carve the hands (o) and feet (p), using mainly the $\frac{1}{2}$ in. chisel; the amount of detail depends on the type and character of the puppet. Insert screw eyes as shown in the drawings.

For the chest and pelvis sections (see fig. 46), cut away any large pieces of wood with a saw and then clear the rest of the wood away with the 1 in. chisel; the $\frac{1}{2}$ in. chisel can be used for finishing off. Drill 2 holes in the lower part of the chest and 2 in the top part of the pelvis as indicated. Drill a large hole at the top of the pelvis to take the neck, and insert a strong screw eye. The body should be loosely linked with short lengths of cord (a). The knots in the cord should be dabbed with Seccotine (Duco Cement).

Drill a large hole in the wooden ball being used for the head, and insert a strong screw eye; it will probably be necessary to hold the screw eye with pliers to do this.

Take the neck and slightly open the screw eye at each end with

Fig. 46 ($\frac{1}{4}$ in.=1 in.)

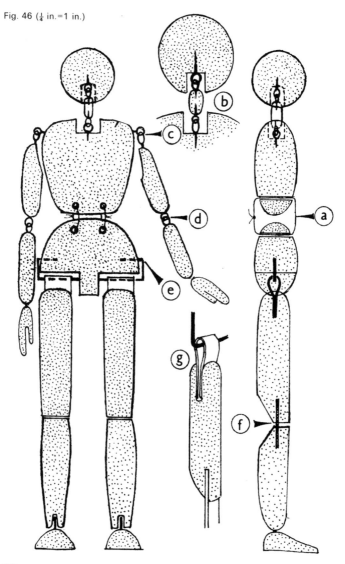

the pliers. Then slip one of the screws through the screw eye in the head and the other into the screw eye in the top of the chest, thus linking the two together, see fig. 46(b). Now close the screw eyes with the pliers.

Insert further screw eyes into the shoulders of the puppet and then link these with the ones in the tops of the arms, (c). Next link the elbow screw eyes (d). For the wrist joint, clip the shafts of two nails to a length equal to the holes drilled through the lower arm, hold the hand with the eye of the screw eye in the slot previously cut in the lower arm, put a little Seccotine (Duco Cement) in the holes and push the clipped nail shaft into the first hole, through the screw eye, and then home into the second hole.

Now fix a strong wire to take the legs. Fig. 46(e) shows how this is done by drilling holes into the sides of the pelvis and a hole through the crotch-piece. The wire can then be threaded through the crotch and bent to shape with a pair of pliers so that the ends can be glued into the holes in the pelvis.

Join the two leg sections together by cutting a piece of leather and sticking it with Seccotine (Duco Cement) into the slots (f), trimming away any excess leather with a blade. Be sure to keep the joint itself free of glue. Allow to dry thoroughly before proceeding any further. The ankle joint follows the same pattern as the wrist. Finally link the legs with the body by cutting strips of leather, hanging them over the wire support, and gluing the two ends into the slots in the tops of the legs (g).

Fig. 47 shows a drawing of the control to be used with this puppet. For the upright holding bar cut 8 in. of 1 in. dowel rod. Cut a head bar (i) 4 in. long and a shoulder prong (j) 3 in. long, and insert these into slots cut in the upright holding bar as shown in the drawing; these should be both glued and screwed in place as otherwise they may work loose and fall off during a performance. Cut a detachable leg bar (k) from a wooden lath 1 in. $\times \frac{1}{4}$ in.; it should be about 10 in. long, and a hole (l) should be drilled in the middle to facilitate its hanging on the cup hook which is inserted into the holding bar (m). To manipulate the legs the bar can be gently rocked on the hook or for bigger movements it can be lifted off the hook and operated freely. Drill holes through the control at (n) and (o) to take the arm wires. These are lengths of wire with loops at the lower end, which are inserted into the control and held in position by bending down the projecting tip (see drawing). The wires are operated by the thumb and one finger which are positioned under the wires in such a way that they can be lifted and lowered while the control is still held by the remaining

Fig. 47 ($\frac{1}{4}$ in.=1 in.)

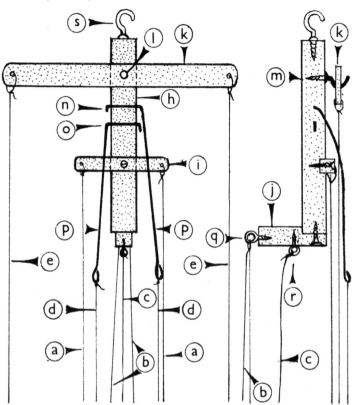

3 fingers. Drill small holes in the ends of the head bar (i), which will eventually take the head strings, and small holes at the ends of the leg bar (k), and insert screw eyes at points (q) and (r). A cup hook should be screwed into the top of the control (s), by which to hang up the puppet.

The basic proportions of the puppet may be varied to alter the character. The figure of the little Negress 'Mary, Mary' (figs. 48/49) is based on dresses of the 1820s. To help this effect the body is carved from balsa wood to a suitable shape (v) omitting the

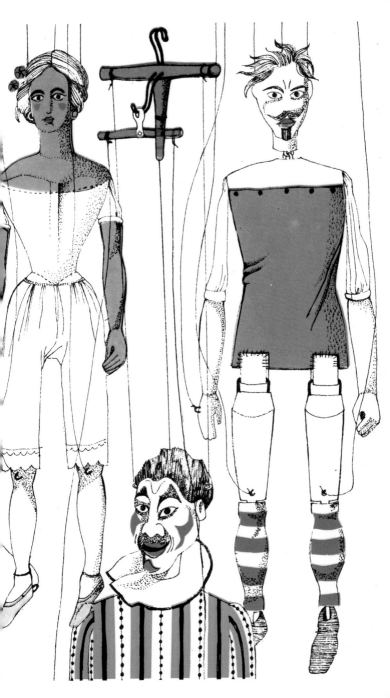

Fig. 48

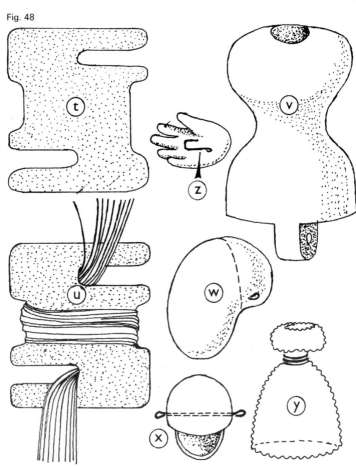

waist joint. A plaster mould is made from a head modelled in plasticine (see page 26), and a hollow cast is then taken in one of the modelling compounds such as Sofenbak, or a mixture can be made of carpenter's glue, fine sawdust and a little plaster of Paris. Remember to grease the mould. Join together as in fig. 48 (w) and push a wire in place (x) to take head strings. Remove the holding wire from a nylon pot scourer and reshape it as (y). This makes the wig. These scourers may be dyed with Dylon or Tintex. A wire (z) is fixed into the hand to facilitate the lifting of the watering can. Dress the puppet before stringing it.

Fig. 49

In figs. 47 and 49 the strings are indicated by the same letters, so by carefully following these two drawings the process should be quite straightforward. The shoulder strings (b) should be attached first; this is a run-through string, starting at one shoulder screw eye, running through the screw eye (q) and being tied off through the other shoulder screw eye. Next fix the head strings (a), one at each side of the head. Make them very slightly slacker than the shoulder strings, as this will give the head a freer movement. The back string (c) needs to be quite taut when the control is in an upright position, so that without any other manipulation than the tipping of the control the puppet will assume a bending position. Leg strings (e) should be long enough to enable the leg bar to be lifted from its retaining hook without any incidental movement of the feet. They should be threaded through the skirt and attached at the knee. An additional foot string (f) is shown in fig. 49.

To attach the hands, drill small holes through the palm and thread the string (d) through, making a substantial knot so that the string does not pull straight through. Tie off the other end to the wire with the hand not quite slack.

Fig. 48(t) shows a winder made from hardboard; this can be used, when transporting puppets, to wind the strings as (u) to prevent entanglement.

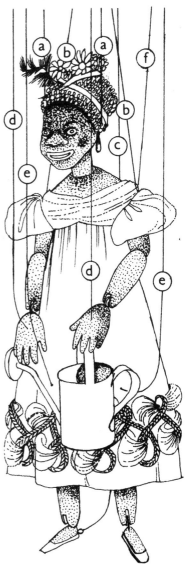

5 Puppets from cardboard or paper

Fig. 50

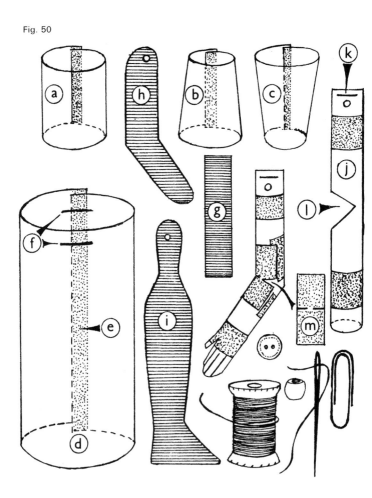

Materials Various kinds of paper and thin cardboard; beads; buttons; paper clips; carpet thread; gumstrip (gummed tape); Seccotine (Duco Cement); paper fasteners; paints; fairly thin sticks or canes for rods.
Tools Ruler; scissors; needles; paint brushes; paper punch (not essential).

Fig. 51

These puppets are very simple to make and, though there are very few movement controls, if the sticks are slightly springy many actions such as walking, bending, swinging and nodding the head can be suggested. Joints should be fairly loose, but all knots in carpet thread should be touched with glue so that they do not come undone.

Fig. 51 shows a basic figure embodying the principal joints, although the individual shapes may be altered. Three different head shapes are shown in fig. 50 (a), (b), (c); these are cylinders or truncated cones; (d) shows the body cylinder, glued as indicated by the dotted area (e). Cut 2 slots (f) just wide enough to take the two neck pieces (g), push these from the inside to the outside and glue as fig. 51 (o). (p). Stick the front of the neck on the outside of the body and the top inside the head to act as a stay.

Cut arms and legs as fig. 50 (h) and (i). The method of attaching them is very simple, following the diagram in fig. 51. Pass the needle through a hole in the button (q) then through the hole in the top of the arm (r) and into the body (s), return the needle through the body about $\frac{1}{4}$ in. from the previous hole, then through the same arm hole and a different hole in the button, then tie off the thread (t).

To fix the leg, thread the needle through the body from the outside, through the hole punched

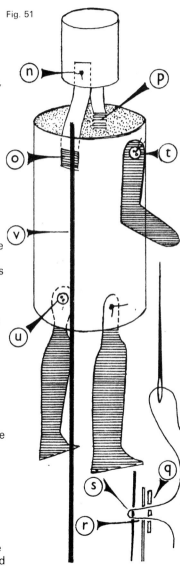

75

Fig. 52

Fig. 53

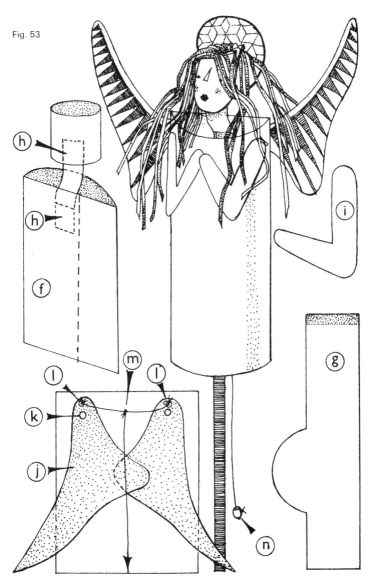

in the top of the leg and then through one of the holes in a button (u), return through a different hole in the button, through the same hole in the leg and make a new hole in the body about $\frac{1}{4}$ in. from the first one in the body, then tie off on the outside. Glue a holding rod into the body cylinder at the back (v). Fig. 52 shows the puppet dressed as an old shepherd. The hat and cloak are of coloured tissue paper (a), this is glued on and should be treated decoratively and not realistically. A staff (b), which can serve as an action rod, is glued to the left hand. The second figure shows one of the three kings; this puppet has a body made from a long cone and the arms and legs, instead of being flat, are made from tubes of paper. Fig. 50 (page 74) shows how these are made: make a paper tube (j), secure with gumstrip (gummed tape) as shown by shaded area. Either staple or glue the top end together and make a hole below (k). For the arms, cut away a V-shaped section (l) and bend the tube so that the cut edges come together. Fasten in this position with a piece of gumstrip (gummed tape) which has been slit at the middle (m). The end of the tube can be cut away to make the hand. The legs are paper tubes without the elbow joint, and with cut paper strips glued in place for feet.

Fig. 54

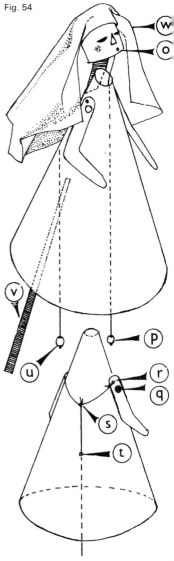

The method of attaching the arms and legs is exactly the same as for the flat types of limb. The cone body may be painted, cuffs are made of tissue paper (c) and the collar (slightly less than a circle) is cut from textured gold paper (d). Beards, wigs etc. may be made from snippets (snips) of thin paper or tissue. The train is of red flock-surfaced paper (e).

Fig. 53 shows a drawing of an angel with movable wings. The body in this case is a half cylinder (f), a small cylinder forms the head (g) and this is joined to the body with a strip of stiff paper glued as shown (h). Cut 2 arms (i); these can be glued so that they do not move, with dabs of glue, or they can be articulated as described in the instructions for the Virgin Mary which follow.

For the wings cut 2 shapes as (j), make holes (k) and with brass paper clips fix them to the back of the body. Thread a needle with carpet thread and pierce the top of the wing and tie off. Carry the thread on to a similar position in the other wing and tie in the same way. Cut the thread. Cut a length of carpet thread and tie round the first thread (m), leaving sufficient to dangle several inches below the bottom of the puppet; tie the end to a bead (n). When the bead is pulled gently downwards the wings will rise. The wings may be painted or decorated with cut paper. A wig is made with strips of tissue paper, and a halo of gold-textured paper is glued at the back of the head. Fix a holding stick inside the back of the puppet.

Finally, fig. 54 shows a puppet figure of the Virgin Mary made from a cone body and a cylinder head, the two being connected by a strip of stiff paper. The head can be made to nod if a string (o) is tied through the chin, threaded through the cone and tied to a bead below (p). Fix the arms to the body with brass paper clips (q), then make small holes with a needle towards the back of the top of the arm (r), tie the thread through this hole, draw the thread across and tie it through a small hole similarly placed in the other arm, and tie off, leaving the thread between the arms a little slack. Tie another thread round the joining thread at (s), push this back through the cone body at (t) and tie to a bead (u). Fix a holding stick (v) in a convenient position. The veil for the head is made from tissue paper cut and glued as necessary (w).

All the figures can be painted and decorated with poster paints, or coloured inks will give an iridescent stained-glass effect. Tissue paper, which is available in a multitude of lovely colours, can be used for details of dress, but the figures should not become cluttered.

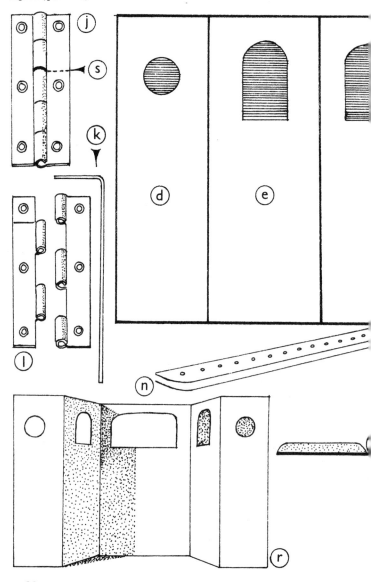

Fig. 55 (½ in.=1 ft)

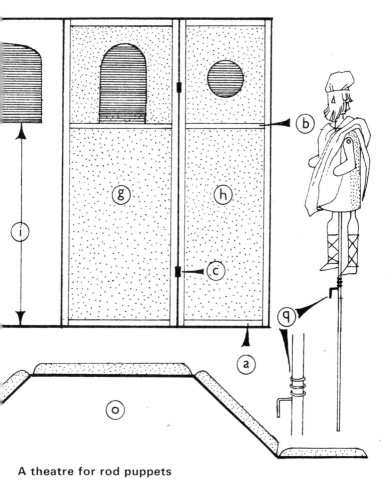

A theatre for rod puppets

Materials Hardboard; thin strips of wood for battens; screws; hinges; wire; paint; Casco glue or Evo-stik Resin W (Elmer's or Sobo).

Tools Saw; 3 ft rule; screwdriver; hack saw; fret saw; paint and glue brushes; drill.

The rod puppets described in this chapter can be operated in a simple stage made of a clothes-horse (collapsible rack for drying clothes) over which strong paper has been pinned with a suitable gap left for the proscenium opening. Alternatively, the puppets may be manipulated above a screen or piece of wood or hardboard, or even a curtain strung across the room at a suitable height. If possible, have a plain curtain or a back-drop painted onto a large sheet of paper or cardboard to provide a backing. This needs to be positioned about three feet behind the operators to allow adequate room for them to be able to move comfortably.

A more elaborate set-up which would give more scope and style to productions, is shown in fig. 55. This is quite easily made by anyone with some basic carpentry skill. The construction is of pieces of hardboard strengthened by battens of $2\frac{1}{2}$ in. × $\frac{1}{2}$ in. wood (a). It is a good idea to make the strengthening batten (b) into a narrow shelf using wood 3 in. × $\frac{1}{2}$ in. as this can then be used to hold puppets which are static. The height of the opening (i) must be determined by the height of the operators; the example given is suitable only for very small children, and should be adjusted so that the heads of the operators are just out of sight.

Cut the hardboard to size and make the openings with a fret saw, then cut the battens accordingly. In the drawing (d), (e) and (f) show the front views of three of the five screens and (g) and (h) the back views. The battens should be glued in position with a casein glue such as Casco (Elmer's glue or Sobo) or with Evo-stik Resin W; they should then be screwed into the hardboard from the front of the screens with screws of a suitable length, at about 12 in. intervals.

The best way to join the screens together is by pin hinges. These can be made from ordinary hinges; fairly large ones should be chosen, say 3 in. With a hack saw cut through the central rod at a gap – diagram (j) at the point (s) – the hinge will then fall into pieces as diagram (l). The two halves should be screwed accurately into position on the screens (c) and when the screens are held together in position a pin made from stout wire (k) is slotted into the channel in the centre and holds the hinge together. The fact that the fit-up can be separated into single screens makes it much easier to store, and also makes it possible to use different combinations of screens. A sketch of the theatre is shown (r) and a plan of the arrangement of screens (o) with the shelves (p). Holes should be drilled in these (n), so that if wire prongs are fitted to the puppet rods (q) the puppets may be left standing in the scene whilst the operator works another figure.

Fig. 56

A CAMEL FROM PAPER AND CARDBOARD

Materials Stiff paper; thin cardboard; tissue paper; buttons; carpet thread or button-hole thread; beads; Bostik (Elmer's glue or Sobo) or Seccotine (Duco Cement); brass paper clips; dowel rod.

Tools Ruler; scissors; needle; paper punch (not essential).

The tube on to which the puppet is built should be made from

Fig. 57

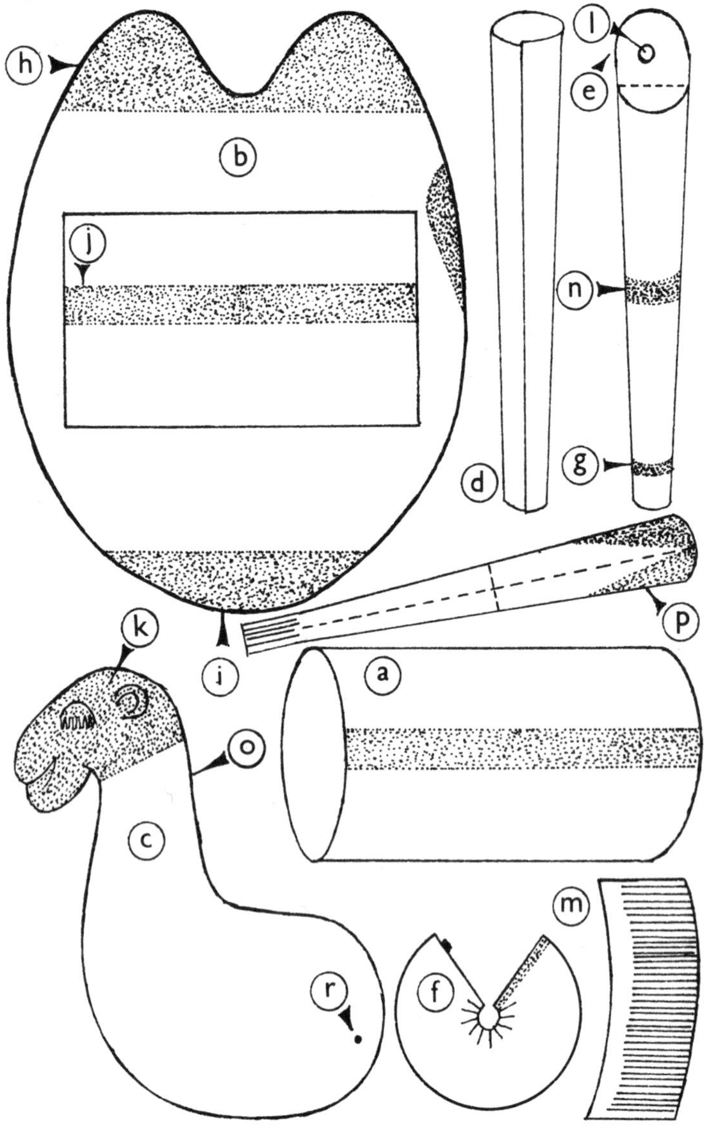

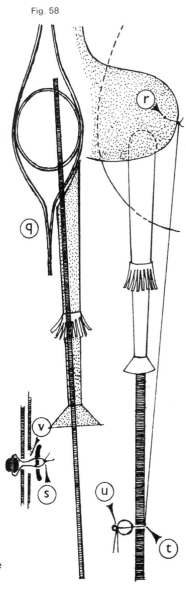

Fig. 58

thin cardboard, fig. 57(a). Make the remaining shapes from firm paper. Cut 2 pieces (b) body, 2 pieces (c) head and neck. Make 4 tapering tubes (d) for legs, cutting away a section at the top (e). Cut 4 cones (f) for feet, snip at top, glue tabs and stick in place at (g). Glue shaded areas (h) and (i) and press 2 sides of body together, inserting tissue paper fringe (m) between humps. When dry, push the cardboard tube between the 2 pieces and glue as (j) on either side. Glue head together at shaded areas (k), inserting a tissue paper mane along neck at (o). Fix all the legs, except one front leg: first punch a good-sized hole at the top of each leg (l), and bend slightly outwards at dotted line. Put a paper fastener into the hole, through the body, and bend the ends back leaving the clip loose enough for the leg to swing easily. *Glue* the remaining front leg in position; when dry, push a length of wooden dowel up the leg and make a hole in the cardboard tube where the rod hits it, push the rod through this hole and through a further hole in the top of the tube, fig. 58(q). Join the neck to the body with a bead and button joint. Thread carpet thread through a button, through a hole in the neck (v), through the body, through a bead and then back again, finishing off with a glued knot (s). The joint should be loose so that the neck moves easily.

Make sure that the mane does not impede the movement of the neck. Cut tissue paper fringes for the knees, fig. 57(m), and stick them in position (n). Cut the tail (p) and fold lengthwise and across on dotted lines; glue in place. To animate the neck pierce a hole at (r) and tie a length of thread through it. Make a hole through the dowel rod, fig. 58(t), and push the thread through it, then through a bead, and tie off round a tiny bead or sequin (u) when the neck is in its lowest position. By pulling the bead the head can be nodded up and down. Add paper eyelids and ears to the head, and set about any painting which is necessary.

SHUTTLECOCK BIRD: A ROD PUPPET

Materials Plastic (or feather) shuttlecock; curtain spring; stiff paper; wooden dowel rod; contact adhesive (cement); carpet thread; beads and sequins.

Tools Pliers with a cutting edge; awl; scissors; drill.

Plastic shuttlecocks are very cheap and can be easily adapted to make puppet birds. Take a length of curtain spring and cut a piece long enough for the legs and the neck (fig. 59). If the wire is very stiff pull with the pliers so that it has more spring. Bend the piece to be used for the neck so that it takes a curve (a), and then insert into the base of the shuttlecock, (b), making a suitable-sized hole with the point of an awl heated in a flame. Make two holes in the side of the shuttlecock in a similar way to take the 2 pieces of spring which form the legs (c). Glue all the pieces of spring into place with Bostik (Elmer's glue or Sobo). Either use a bead for the head, or model a bird's head onto the end of the neck with modelling compound or papier mâché, (d). Wires with beads or sequins on the ends can be stuck into the head for decoration, a faceted sequin makes the eye. A frill of paper makes a ruff for the neck (e) and little scraps of foil can be added to the body of the bird to give sparkle (f). Alternatively it could be covered with tissue paper feathers.

Drive a length of wire into a hole in the top of a piece of dowel leaving about 1 in. protruding, and push this into one of the spring legs, gluing if necessary (g); cut a length of similar wire and insert in the other leg (h), bend the wire at a right angle as shown in the drawing and pass through a hole which has been drilled in the rod (i). Wind the wire round the rod to make it secure. Drill another hole in the rod (j) and put a wire through this as shown in the diagram. Tie a thread to the tail, pass through the

Fig. 59

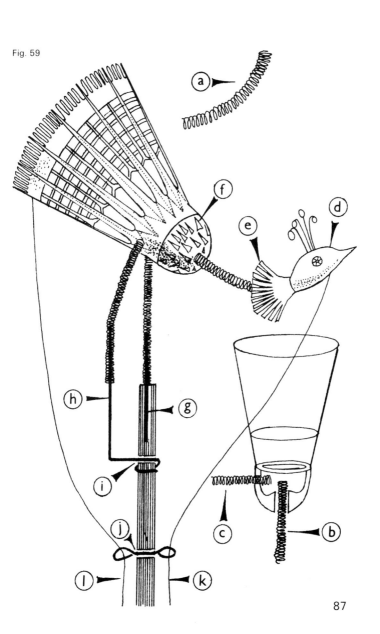

87

wire loop (l) and tie off to a bead; make a hole in the head and tie another thread through it and pass through the other wire loop (k), again tie off to a bead; be sure the threads are long enough not to restrict each other's movements.

SHUTTLECOCK BIRD: STRING PUPPET

Materials Shuttlecock; beads; carpet thread; dowel; tissue paper; wire; elastic; small brass rings; screw eyes; Tapwata paste or acrylic medium; Bostik (Elmer's glue or Sobo).
Tools Scissors; pliers; paste brush; awl; needle.

Take 2 lengths of wire and bend as fig. 60(m) to make the two legs, cover these with strips of tissue paper dipped in Tapwata paste or acrylic medium, leaving the loop clear (n). Put 2 wires through the base of the shuttlecock, making the holes with the point of an awl which has been heated in a flame, also pass a thread through the tip of the shuttlecock (o). Make a head, which may be based on a bead or modelled with any modelling compound, such as Plastone, which harden without firing. Insert a thread into the head whilst it is being constructed, also incorporate a screw eye into the neck. Thread some beads on to the neck thread (p) and then tie off into the neck screw eye. Slip the leg loops onto the wire hooks protruding from the sides of the shuttlecock. Make a tissue paper ruff for the bird's neck and stick to the head (q).

Now construct the control from a length of $\frac{3}{4}$ in. dowel, drill a hole vertically (r) and a hole horizontally (s). Insert a screw eye at the back of the bar (t). Make a wire triangle as (u) which passes through a screw eye (v), connect the feet to this with threads as shown in the drawing. Connect threads from the body to a wire passing through the hole drilled through the control at (s). Tie a length of hat elastic to the screw eye (t) and fasten the other end to a small brass ring, (w). Join the ring to the tail with a length of carpet thread. Tie another piece of hat elastic to a bead,, pass it through the hole previously drilled at (r), tie off to a small brass ring (x). Join the thread already inserted into the head to the same brass ring.

By pulling on the ring the head may be lowered, by raising the bead the head may be raised. To lower the tail, pull the tail ring. Experiment with the leg control to discover how the bird can be made to hop and walk.

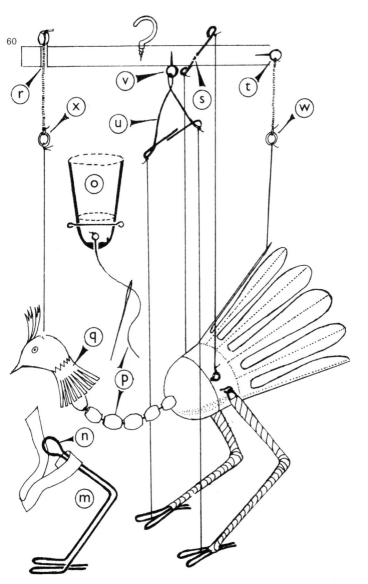

6 Some notes on dressing puppets

The first essential in dressing puppets is that the clothes should in no way impede the movements. Secondly it should be clearly recognized that clothing a puppet is not like dressing a doll – the garments are not miniature clothes, just as puppets are not tiny people. Although the puppet is usually dressed when the figure is joined together but not attached to the control and is therefore reminiscent of a doll, it must never be thought of in this way. The costume is an integral part of the construction of the puppet and so is just another process in its creation.

Depending on the kind of puppet, it may be necessary partly to stitch the costume before putting it on to the puppet; sometimes the fabric may actually be stitched to the puppet, or it may be best to glue it in place with a latex or rubber-based glue or contact adhesive (cement). Unless there is a specific reason for the costume being stiff, soft fabrics such as jersey, particularly cotton and celanese jersey, are best as they move easily and take pleasing and small-scale folds. The scale of the material is very important indeed: coarse bulky weaves, stiff satins, brocades etc, not only move badly but look out of key. If the character calls for the kind of design found in a brocade or a furnishing (drapery or upholstery) fabric, or in a stiff striped silk, then the pattern will have to be reproduced in some way on a more suitable fabric. Ways of doing this are discussed later. Variation of textures is important and the introduction of rough, coarse but *soft* materials such as knitted dish-cloths can be very valuable; they can be dyed very easily in a small quantity of dye, such as Dylon or Tintex, either to an even result or roughly so that the colour is slightly broken. Different kinds of net may be used for the same purpose; these are often improved by soaking in hot water to remove some of the dressing. Small quantities of velvet may occasionally be useful but should be used with discretion, as although the texture is pleasing the weight and scale are difficult to manage.

Collect in a bag any scraps of lace, cord, braids, plain and frilled edgings. Small feathers and bits of ostrich feather, skeins of silk, wool (yarn) and raffia will all come in useful. Also keep a box for sequins, beads, buttons, fancy-headed pins and tacks so that there is always a selection of materials at hand.

Good use can be made of patterned materials in dressing puppets, particularly small printed designs, or tiny ginghams and spot patterns. Sometimes a suitable material can be found, but there are times when it is more satisfactory to print the fabric by some simple method such as a potato print or stencil, the method chosen depending on the kind of pattern required. If a

Fig. 61

very simple spot motif is needed this can be produced by a stick print; use a length of dowel (b) or a piece of square sectioned wood (c), paint the end with designer's colour or poster colour, and print the material with this. To print a pattern of small circles cut a length of bamboo and use this, (a). For slightly more detailed patterns a potato cut makes a satisfactory method. Slice a potato in half with a clean, level cut and then use a Stanley blade to cut the design; (d) shows a pattern still retaining the outside shape of the potato, (e) shows how this may be done away with altogether. Use an ordinary water-colour brush to put the paint on to the printing surface. A little Tapwata paste or acrylic medium added to the poster paint will give it body and stop it from spreading on the material.

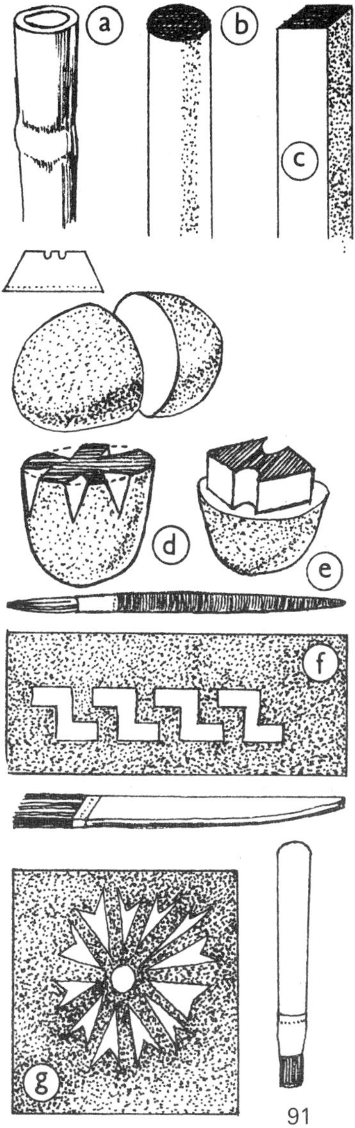

Stencilling is another way of making patterns, and may be used for spot patterns or borders. Oiled stencil paper is the best to use, but failing this thin hard-surfaced cardboard should be used. The design should be cut with a sharp knife or blade with the stencil paper on a hard surface such as a sheet of glass; fig. 61 (f) shows a border pattern and (g) a spot motif. Poster paint or designer's colour may be used; care should be taken that they do not get too runny or they will leak under the stencil and blur the pattern. Use either a lining fitch or a stiff-bristled stencil brush to apply the paint with a dabbing action.

Alternatively paint may be sprayed through the stencil with a mouth spray, fig. 62(h), or an aerosol paint spray is very efficient. Either kind of spray may be used to shade or vary the tones on costumes and this can be very effective.

Tie dyeing produces very pleasing textures in materials, and is simply carried out. Tightly bind parts of the fabric with string or thread (i) and dip the material in dye. Allow to dry before untying. Another variation of this method is to tie the threads round beads or seeds; this can be done with beads of similar size at equidistant intervals for a regular effect (j) or erratically with different-sized beads for a more casual effect.

Appliqué is useful for more stylized costumes, for clowns, harlequins and for all kinds of formal decoration. One of the main advantages of this method of decoration is that it can combine many different textures. Only small quantities of fabric are usually required so that there is usually little difficulty in finding materials. If a number of similar pieces will be needed it is advisable to cut a template from thin cardboard and, with a sharp soft pencil, to trace round the shape using either the shape cut out (k) or the shape left in the card (l), depending on the

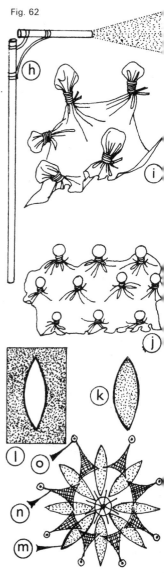

Fig. 62

type of shape being cut. Intricate shapes are less likely to tear if the latter method is used.

The example shown in fig. 62 shows felt shapes (m) overlapped with coarse net shapes (n) with the addition of sequins (o) for sparkle. Copydex or Sobo are the best adhesives to use for fabrics, but Bostik or Elmer's glue are also satisfactory; care must be taken to prevent the appliqué becoming stiff and inhibiting the movements of the puppet.

String is another useful textural material which may be glued or stitched into place and then sprayed lightly with paint. It can be combined with painted decoration as fig. 63(p) or encrusted with beads and sequins for a really rich effect (q); and (r) shows how it is used to give interest to a Mexican hat made of cardboard.

These notes can only point the way; the possibilities of decoration are wide and there is plenty of scope for experiment.

Fig. 63

93

Fig. 64

Some ways of making wigs

The drawings on this page show various ways of treating hair styles with different materials. (a) Foam rubber clipped into shape and painted with F.E.V., emulsion, or acrylic paint (it takes a long time to dry). (b) A wooden Dutch doll turned into a puppet; a topknot of black nylon crin or stiff net is added to the painted hair. (c) Carved wooden head of a savage with a strip of carpet (cut with a razor blade) stuck down the middle of the head. (d) A straggly wig made from strands of wool (yarn) glued into place. (e) The basic shape of the wig is modelled with the shape of the head; on to this are stuck loops of coarse string, bound together at the top and the ends unravelled with a needle. (See also instructions for individual puppets.)

7 A glove puppet theatre

Fig. 65

Materials Hardboard; $1\frac{1}{2}$ in. $\times \frac{1}{2}$ in. dowel; an old picture frame; 4 hinges (3 in.); screw eyes and screws; double track spring curtain rod and strings; Casco glue (Elmer's glue or Sobo) or Evo-stik Resin W; 2 lead weights; carpet thread; Rufflette tape; felt for pelmet (valances); jersey materials for curtain; emulsion paint.
Tools Saw; screwdriver; awl; 3 ft rule; hack saw; glue and paint brushes; scissors; needle and cotton thread.

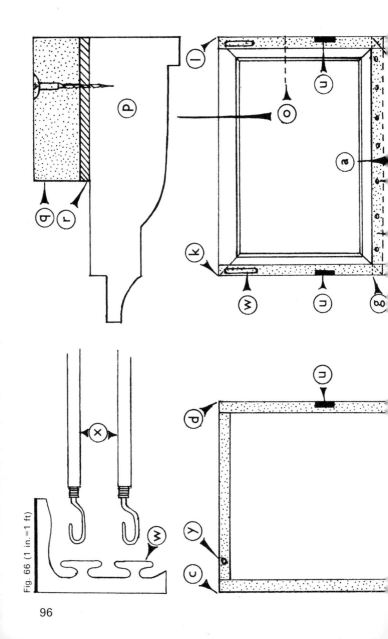

Fig. 66 (1 in. = 1 ft)

96

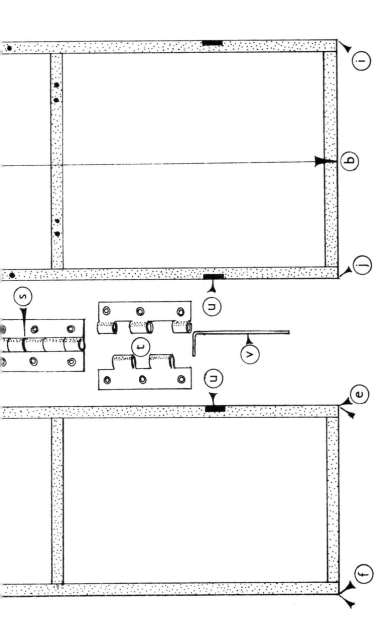

This theatre is simply constructed from hardboard and wooden battens (strips). It is essential before beginning work to establish the height of the tallest operator and to adjust the measurement (a)–(b) accordingly: it should be sufficient to mask the heads of those working behind the scenes.

Cut 2 pieces of hardboard for the side wings of the theatre (c)–(d)–(e)–(f), and one piece for the front; the width of the front section must also be adjusted to the width of the picture frame available. It is wisest to draw both side wings and front carefully on paper so that the measurements are quite clear before starting work on the construction. The hardboard for the front section needs to be (g)–(h)–(i)–(j). Cut 4 long battens (thin strips of wood) from $1\frac{1}{2}$ in. × $\frac{1}{2}$ in. wood, each equal to the length (c)–(f); these are for the side wings. Two similar lengths form the long battens for the front (j)–(k) and (l)–(i). Then cut the cross battens as indicated on the drawing, being sure that they fit closely between the uprights. Fix these in place with either Casco (Elmer's glue or Sobo) or Evo-stik Resin W and insert screws into the battens from the front of the screens, i.e. through the hardboard into the wood. Glue the batten (m) into position. Place the picture frame in position and screw through the batten into the frame from the back of the work (n); screws should be at intervals of about 6 in.

To complete the fixing of the frame, look at the enlarged draw-ing of a section taken at (o). Between the frame (p) and the batten (q) it is necessary to insert a strip of hardboard (r), to bring the level of the picture frame and the surrounding screen into alignment. Having done this, glue the batten to the hardboard and then secure the frame in position by putting screws through the batten and the hardboard into the frame.

The best way to join the three sections together is by using pin hinges; the theatre can then be stored away in 3 flat sections. To make the hinges, take ordinary hinges and with a hack saw cut through the central pin at one of the intersections (s); the hinge will then fall into two parts (t). These should be screwed into place very accurately on the upright battens (u). Pins should be made from thick wire (v). When the sections of the theatre are held in position, the wire pins can be dropped into the channel left through the middle of hinges, and this will hold the theatre together.

Although not essential, it is nice to have a curtain which opens and closes. This is easily achieved by buying a double track spring curtain rod set from Woolworths. These are very inexpen-

Fig. 67

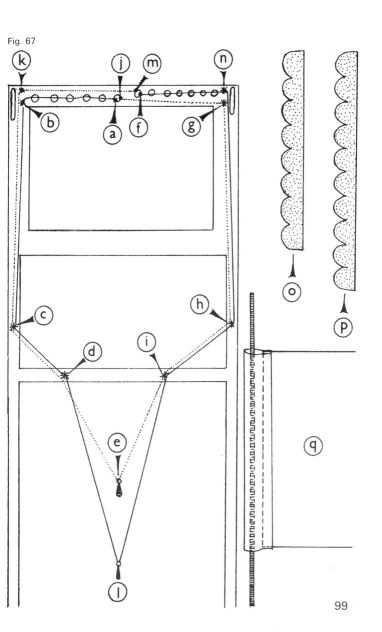

99

sive. The brackets which take the expanding wire, fig. 66(w), are fixed in place as indicated and the wires themselves cut to length if necessary and hooked into position (x). Cut the curtains from the chosen material, jersey for preference, being certain to allow enough fullness, and allow an extra few inches for length. Stitch the Rufflette tape in position, and hook the rings on to the tape. Thread the curtains on to the curtain wires. Now follow fig. 67. Take a good length of carpet thread or thin cord and tie it to curtain ring (a), thread back through the rings and then through screw eyes at points (b), (c) and (d), leaving a good length spare. Now tie another length of thread through curtain ring (f), thread back through the rings and through screw eyes at points (n), (h) and (i). Leave an equal amount of spare thread, and tie both loose ends to a lead weight (l) (the kind that is used for fishing). This link thread opens the curtain when the weight is pulled. To attach the closing cord tie a thread at the point marked (m), pass it through a screw eye at (k), through screw eyes (c) and (d) and leave a long loose end. Start with a fresh thread at (j) and pass through a screw eye at (g), then through screw eyes (h) and (i). Equalize the lengths of the two loose ends and tie to another lead weight (e). Test to see that the cords are not too tight to fully open and close the curtains, and that the threads and weights are not on the floor.

Cut two felt pelmets (valances), one for the top of the picture frame on the inside (o), and one for the lower edge of the frame on the front (p). (See also fig. 65.)

Paint the theatre with emulsion paint, using a colour which will not distract too much from the puppets and any scenery which is being used. Other decorations such as flags can be added and perhaps a little painted decoration on the front.

A plain curtain or painted back-cloth or card may be hung at the back of the booth; to do this drill holes to take a rod at the back of the side wings, fig. 66(y). Sew a channel along the top of any cloths or curtains to be used, or, if using cardboard, glue a folded length of material along the top, fig. 67(q). To put the back-cloth in place, push a rod through the hole in one side wing, thread it through the channel in the cloth and then through the hole in the other side wing.

8   Some notes on scenery

The settings in which puppets are operated should usually be very simple so that the character and actions of the puppets will be seen to full advantage. Often a perfectly plain backing in an appropriate colour is all that is necessary – either a piece of plain coloured material or a canvas cloth which is first primed and then painted with scenic colours or emulsion paint. The paint gives a texture and quality which is both theatrical and pleasing. The cloth may be painted with variations of tone and texture by using brush strokes, or scummelling rather dry paint into the basic colour, by dribbling, spattering and spraying. Cloths may also be painted with dyes and this will give a very vivid and translucent effect.

The best material for cloths for the puppet stage is unbleached calico which is both cheap and easily obtainable in a number of widths. Prime the cloths with glue size: half a pound of size should be soaked in a little cold water and later dissolved in about half a gallon of boiling water. Stir until thoroughly dissolved and then apply to the cloth stretched on newspaper on the floor. The cloth will tighten as it dries to give a good surface on which to work. For painting use dry powder colours mixed to a creamy consistency with liquid size; if too little size is used the paint will rub off, if the solution is too strong it will crack. The paint will jelly when it gets cold but this can be remedied by *very gentle* reheating. For small areas poster paints and designer's colours may be used, but they are much more expensive. For small stages, backings may be painted on stiff paper or cardboard with a batten (thin strip of wood) pinned top and bottom to prevent curling. Any design painted on the cloth should echo the mood and style of the all-important puppets, otherwise it will detract from rather than add to the performance.

Apertures may be cut in the cloth, such as arches, doors, windows or the spaces between the branches of trees, and puppets may appear in these to give an extra dimension to the action, performing in front of and behind the cloth. Their entrances and exits can be made more varied with the use of these spaces.

Battens across the top of the theatre may be used for hanging small pieces of scenery such as a decoratively-painted sun or moon, or a string of flags. Care should be taken that these pieces of scenery do not impede the action.

Growing scenery is possible in the puppet theatre. For rod puppets a plant or tree can be constructed on dowel rod and made to grow by slowly pushing it from below. For string puppets, the plant will have to be drawn up from above, which necessitates a weighty base on which to mount the construction – a box filled with lead dress weights or lead shot can be used, fig. 68(o); to this a length of round elastic is fixed, with leaves and flowers attached to it at intervals. Suspend the top flower from a control made of dowel with two lengths of carpet thread (p). Two strings will prevent the plant from spinning round.

Leaves can be made from felt stiffened with shellac or from vilene or several layers of net stitched together; if they are too stiff and prickly they may interfere with other puppet strings.

The sunflower in fig. 68 has felt petals, slightly stiffened, and glued to a plywood circle with a contact adhesive. The centre is raised with a modelling paste such as Plastone, and then smeared with Bostik (Elmer's glue or Sobo) and sprinkled liberally with tiny bugle beads or sequins.

If a hook (q) is fixed into the top of the control large enough to hook over the back cloth, the plant can be hung up when it has reached its full height, leaving the operator free to work another puppet.

Fig. 68

Further reading

Dolls and Puppets Max Von Boehn, Harrap, London 1932
Histoire Generale des Marionettes Jacques Chenais, Bordas 1947
Your Puppetry John Wright, Sylvan Press, London 1951
Everybody's Marionette Book H. W. Whanslaw, Wells Gardner,
   Darton & Co, London 1948
Specialised Puppetry H. W. Whanslaw, Wells Gardner, Darton &
   Co, London 1948
History of the English Puppet Theatre George Speaight, Harrap,
   London 1955
Mr Punch Philip John Stead, Evans, London 1950
Puppetry Today Helen Binyon, Studio Vista, London, and Watson-
   Guptill, New York 1966
My Profession Sergei Obraztsov, Foreign Languages Publishing
   House, Moscow
Introducing Puppetry Peter Fraser, Batsford, London, and
   Watson-Guptill, New York 1968
Presenting Marionettes Susan French, Reinhold, New York 1964
Folk Plays for Puppets You can Make Tom H. Tichenor, Abingdon,
   New York 1959